Recruiting and Retaining Adult Students

Peter S. Cookson, *Editor*
Pennsylvania State University

NEW DIRECTIONS FOR CONTINUING EDUCATION
RALPH G. BROCKETT, *Editor-in-Chief*
University of Tennessee, Knoxville

ALAN B. KNOX, *Consulting Editor*
University of Wisconsin

Number 41, Spring 1989

Paperback sourcebooks in
The Jossey-Bass Higher Education Series

Jossey-Bass Inc., Publishers
San Francisco • London

Peter S. Cookson (ed.).
Recruiting and Retaining Adult Students.
New Directions for Continuing Education, no. 41.
San Francisco: Jossey-Bass, 1989.

New Directions for Continuing Education
Ralph G. Brockett, *Editor-in-Chief*
Alan B. Knox, *Consulting Editor*

Copyright © 1989 by Jossey-Bass Inc., Publishers
and
Jossey-Bass Limited

Copyright under International, Pan American, and Universal Copyright Conventions. All rights reserved. No part of this issue may be reproduced in any form—except for brief quotation (not to exceed 500 words) in a review or professional work—without permission in writing from the publishers.

New Directions for Continuing Education is published quarterly by Jossey-Bass Inc., Publishers (publication number USPS 493-930). Second-class postage paid at San Francisco, California, and at additional mailing offices. POSTMASTER: Send address changes to Jossey-Bass Inc., Publishers, 350 Sansome Street, San Francisco, California 94104.

Editorial correspondence should be sent to the Editor-in-Chief, Ralph G. Brockett, Dept. of Technological and Adult Education, University of Tennessee, 402 Claxton Addition, Knoxville, Tennessee 37996-3400.

Library of Congress Catalog Card Number LC 85-644750

International Standard Serial Number ISSN 0195-2242

International Standard Book Number ISBN 1-55542-860-6

Cover art by WILLI BAUM

Manufactured in the United States of America. Printed on acid-free paper.

Ordering Information

The paperback sourcebooks listed below are published quarterly and can be ordered either by subscription or single copy.

Subscriptions cost $52.00 per year for institutions, agencies, and libraries. Individuals can subscribe at the special rate of $39.00 per year *if payment is by personal check.* (Note that the full rate of $52.00 applies if payment is by institutional check, even if the subscription is designated for an individual.) Standing orders are accepted.

Single copies are available at $12.95 when payment accompanies order. (California, New Jersey, New York, and Washington, D.C., residents please include appropriate sales tax.) For billed orders, cost per copy is $12.95 plus postage and handling.

Substantial discounts are offered to organizations and individuals wishing to purchase bulk quantities of Jossey-Bass sourcebooks. Please inquire.

Please note that these prices are for the calendar year 1989 and are subject to change without notice. Also, some titles may be out of print and therefore not available for sale.

To ensure correct and prompt delivery, all orders must give either the *name of an individual* or an *official purchase order number.* Please submit your order as follows:

Subscriptions: specify series and year subscription is to begin.
Single Copies: specify sourcebook code (such as, CE1) and first two words of title.

Mail orders for United States and Possessions, Latin America, Canada, Japan, Australia, and New Zealand to:
  Jossey-Bass Inc., Publishers
  350 Sansome Street
  San Francisco, California 94104

Mail orders for all other parts of the world to:
  Jossey-Bass Limited
  28 Banner Street
  London EC1Y 8QE

New Directions for Continuing Education Series
Ralph G. Brockett, *Editor-in-Chief*
Alan B. Knox, *Consulting Editor*

CE1 *Enhancing Proficiencies of Continuing Educators,* Alan B. Knox
CE2 *Programming for Adults Facing Mid-Life Change,* Alan B. Knox
CE3 *Assessing the Impact of Continuing Education,* Alan B. Knox

CE4	*Attracting Able Instructors of Adults,* M. Alan Brown, Harlan G. Copeland
CE5	*Providing Continuing Education by Media and Technology,* Martin N. Chamberlain
CE6	*Teaching Adults Effectively,* Alan B. Knox
CE7	*Assessing Educational Needs of Adults,* Floyd C. Pennington
CE8	*Reaching Hard-to-Reach Adults,* Gordon G. Darkenwald, Gordon A. Larson
CE9	*Strengthening Internal Support for Continuing Education,* James C. Votruba
CE10	*Advising and Counseling Adult Learners,* Frank R. DiSilvestro
CE11	*Continuing Education for Community Leadership,* Harold W. Stubblefield
CE12	*Attracting External Funds for Continuing Education,* John H. Buskey
CE13	*Leadership Strategies for Meeting New Challenges,* Alan B. Knox
CE14	*Programs for Older Adults,* Morris A. Okun
CE15	*Linking Philosophy and Practice,* Sharan B. Merriam
CE16	*Creative Financing and Budgeting,* Travis Shipp
CE17	*Materials for Teaching Adults: Selection, Development, and Use,* John P. Wilson
CE18	*Strengthening Connections Between Education and Performance,* Stanley M. Grabowski
CE19	*Helping Adults Learn How to Learn,* Robert M. Smith
CE20	*Educational Outreach to Select Adult Populations,* Carol E. Kasworm
CE21	*Meeting Educational Needs of Young Adults,* Gordon G. Darkenwald, Alan B. Knox
CE22	*Designing and Implementing Effective Workshops,* Thomas J. Sork
CE23	*Realizing the Potential of Interorganizational Cooperation,* Hal Beder
CE24	*Evaluation for Program Improvement,* David Deshler
CE25	*Self-Directed Learning: From Theory to Practice,* Stephen Brookfield
CE26	*Involving Adults in the Educational Process,* Sandra H. Rosenblum
CE27	*Problems and Prospects in Continuing Professional Education,* Ronald M. Cervero, Craig L. Scanlan
CE28	*Improving Conference Design and Outcomes,* Paul J. Ilsley
CE29	*Personal Computers and the Adult Learner,* Barry Heermann
CE30	*Experiential and Simulation Techniques for Teaching Adults,* Linda H. Lewis
CE31	*Marketing Continuing Education,* Hal Beder
CE32	*Issues in Adult Career Counseling,* Juliet V. Miller, Mary Lynne Musgrove
CE33	*Responding to the Educational Needs of Today's Workplace,* Ivan Charner, Catherine A. Rolzinski
CE34	*Technologies for Learning Outside the Classroom,* John A. Niemi, Dennis D. Gooler
CE35	*Competitive Strategies for Continuing Education,* Clifford Baden
CE36	*Continuing Education in the Year 2000,* Ralph G. Brockett
CE37	*China: Lessons from Practice,* Wang Maorong, Lin Weihua, Sun Shilu, Fang Jing
CE38	*Enhancing Staff Development in Diverse Settings,* Victoria J. Marsick
CE39	*Addressing the Needs of Returning Women,* Linda H. Lewis
CE40	*Britain: Policy and Practice in Continuing Education,* Peter Jarvis

Contents

Editor's Notes 1
Peter S. Cookson

1. **Recruiting and Retaining Adult Students:** 3
A Practice Perspective
Peter S. Cookson
Effective implementation of the processes of recruiting and retaining adult students is vital to the survival and growth of continuing education programs.

2. **Recruiting and Retaining Adult Students:** 13
An Organizational Theory Perspective
Peter S. Cookson
Two examples of organizational theory provide a framework within which the organizational tasks required to initiate and maintain continuing education programs can be conceptualized.

3. **Recruiting and Retaining Adult Students:** 23
A Marketing Perspective
William S. Griffith
The recruitment and the retention of adults in educational programs are influenced by a program planning perspective that resembles modern marketing.

4. **Recruiting and Retaining Adult Students** 35
in Continuing Professional Education
Brandt W. Pryor
This chapter examines how adults decide whether to participate in continuing professional education programs.

5. **Recruiting and Retaining Adult Students in Higher Education** 49
Jovita Martin Ross
It appears that adult undergraduates are here to stay, and institutions of higher education have become more responsive to their needs. This chapter reports on some successful approaches to recruiting, admitting, and retaining the members of this student population.

6. **Recruiting and Retaining Adult Students** 63
in Continuing Higher Education
Joe F. Donaldson
Recruitment and retention strategies in continuing higher education must consider both organizational and programmatic approaches and focus on the subtleties of learners' participation patterns.

7. Recruiting and Retaining Adult Students in Literacy and ABE   79
Larry G. Martin
Effective recruiting and retention strategies for adult literacy programs require systematic efforts.

8. Recruiting and Retaining Adult Students in Distance Education   89
Michael G. Moore
The phenomenon of dropout that once plagued correspondence education can be reduced in modern distance education systems by careful recruitment techniques and counseling strategies.

9. Recruiting and Retaining Adult Students in HRD   99
Diane Roemer Yarosz
Tying training programs directly to a corporation's management system, such as strategic planning and succession planning, minimizes the need for human resource professionals to focus on recruitment and retention.

10. Recruiting and Retaining Adult Students: Guidelines for Practice   107
Peter S. Cookson
This chapter summarizes the effective recruitment and retention practices presented in preceding chapters.

Index   111

Editor's Notes

Programs of sponsored, planned adult learning involve a bewildering diversity not only of organizational contexts but also of participants, goals and objectives, and methods and techniques. Because adult learning is a largely voluntary enterprise, we cannot assume that adult students will participate automatically. In the main, adults choose for themselves to become students. It is therefore incumbent on institutional sponsors to design and implement strategies that will encourage men and women not only to enter their educational programs but to stay until they have completed those programs. Both the inception and the durability of educational programs for adults depend on how effectively program planners recruit and retain adult learners.

The purpose of this sourcebook is to suggest concrete, practical strategies for increasing the effectiveness of the processes of recruitment and retention of adult students in a variety of institutional and agency contexts. The first three chapters examine these processes in terms of general principles of continuing education practice, organizational theory, and specific marketing strategies. The remaining chapters highlight recruitment and retention strategies in such diverse areas of practice as continuing professional education, higher education for older adult students, continuing higher education, adult basic education, distance education, and human resource development.

Lest practitioners in any one kind of institutional setting dismiss the relevance of experience in other educational settings, I cite what Cyril O. Houle (1972) calls "the basic unity of process" that underlies all forms of purposive and systematic learning by adults. Thus, experiences obtained in organizational settings different from one's own can still be instructive for one's own educational practice.

The first three chapters afford an overview of the literature and practice on adult recruitment and retention across the entire spectrum of continuing education. Chapter One describes the recruitment and retention of adult students as two related steps in systematic program design. Chapter Two explicates these steps in light of two organizational theories. In Chapter Three, Griffith focuses on recruitment practices from the standpoint of marketing principles and strategies.

The next three chapters examine some activities often conducted under the purview of higher education institutions. In Chapter Four, Pryor presents a theoretical model that implicates recruitment and retention practices in professional continuing education. His model has potential explanatory power for understanding these same processes across the spectrum of sponsored adult and continuing education. In Chapter Five, Ross discusses the participation patterns of adult students in higher education in the 1980s, projects the likely patterns to the year 2000, and describes recruitment and retention strategies that higher education institutions can implement to respond effectively to the predicted trends. In Chapter Six, Donaldson reviews organizing principles that can guide continuing higher education practitioners in recruiting new participants and in increasing the likelihood that enrollees will continue to participate.

The next three chapters discuss recruiting and retaining processes that often occur outside of higher education settings. In Chapter Seven, Martin touches on procedures that organizers of adult basic education can use to attract students and assist them to persist until their goals are achieved. In Chapter Eight, Moore explains that the separation between learners and instructors in distance education makes counseling as well as other sources of support during the process of learning vital to effective recruitment and retention. In Chapter Nine, Yarosz explains that, as long as human resource development programs are designed in accordance with actual organizational goals and individuals' career goals and aspirations, the need for recruitment strategies will be minimized.

Every chapter in this sourcebook cites references to theoretical frameworks that help to conceptualize the recruitment and retention processes as well as research findings and reports from successful programs. In Chapter Ten, the editor reviews the major concepts discussed in the previous chapters and notes the implications for practice. The summary chapter includes two sets of guidelines. The implicit agenda for action is applicable to a variety of continuing education practitioners, irrespective of their institutional or agency affiliation.

Thinking through the processes of recruiting and retaining adult students has been a fulfilling, albeit challenging, experience. I wish to thank the authors and two editors-in-chief—Gordon G. Darkenwald and his successor Ralph G. Brockett—whose devotion to adult students and to those who teach and plan for and with them is exemplified by their contributions to this sourcebook.

Peter S. Cookson
Editor

Reference

Houle, C. O. *The Design of Education*. San Francisco: Jossey-Bass, 1972.

Peter S. Cookson is associate professor of adult education and professor-in-charge of the Adult Education Program at Pennsylvania State University.

Effective implementation of the processes of recruiting and retaining adult students is vital to the survival and growth of continuing education programs.

Recruiting and Retaining Adult Students: A Practice Perspective

Peter S. Cookson

From the perspective of the continuing education practitioner, recruitment and retention are probably the two most important steps in the program planning process. An education or training program may be designed according to the most exacting criteria derived from a thorough assessment of learning needs; it may employ the most expert and competent instructors, the most sensitive facilitators of adult learning; it may provide for appropriate formative and summative evaluation of the outcomes of learning. But, unless it is successful both in attracting adult participants and in motivating them to stay with the program, there simply will be no program.

The term *recruitment* refers to the step of inducing prospective adult students to participate in a program of systematic learning. Such inducement is effected by the direct or indirect transmission of information about the program to prospective learners by the program's sponsor. The decision of prospective learners to participate can be regarded as a positive behavioral response to both the content and the process of the information that they receive about the program.

The term *retention* refers to participation that continues until the program is completed. Thus, retention can be defined as the capacity of a continuing education program to transform the decision to participate into continuing participation. Retention can also be regarded as a positive behavioral response on the part of adult learners to such distinctive features as the continuing education program and the organizational sponsor as well as to life context external to the program.

What do continuing educators do to recruit adult students? What must continuing educators do if their programs are to retain adult students? What are the critical factors in effective recruiting and retention of adult students?

There are numerous ways of answering these questions. The normative literature on program planning in continuing education can yield valuable prescriptions about specific practice appropriate to a wide diversity of continuing education programs. Narrative accounts of the experiences and practices of specific institutions yield valuable examples that resourceful practitioners can emulate. The literature on recruitment and retention-related phenomena affords additional insights (Darkenwald, 1981, 1982). This chapter reviews the basic principles of recruitment and retention as program planning concerns.

Recruitment and Retention Practices

The ways in which continuing education practitioners come to terms with the recruitment and retention of adult students are as innumerable as the field is diverse. For forms of continuing education wherein participation is obligatory—for example, safety training for operatives or shop floor stewards in an industrial plant, routine staff development for nursing practitioners in a hospital, preservice training for new hires—recruitment may be either negligible or nonexistent. For forms of continuing education in which participation is voluntary—for example, courses or conferences organized by the continuing education unit of a higher education institution, graduate-level courses for employed business executives, optional correspondence courses for military personnel—recruitment and retention practices affect the very existence and vitality of the continuing education program. In practice, recruitment activities and retention activities often complement and overlap one another. In this chapter, these activities are discussed separately.

Recruiting Adult Students

As already noted, recruitment can be viewed as a step in the overall program design aimed at inducing voluntary adult learners to affiliate with a program of systematic learning. Before adult students can initiate their involvement in an education program, they must become aware of the program and form favorable dispositions toward the prospect of personal involvement. The organizational sponsor of the continuing education program must therefore be concerned not only about the content of information about the program but also about the process whereby such information is communicated, either directly or indirectly.

Many of the program planning models in the literature on continuing education seem to take the participation of adult learners for granted and pay little attention to the mechanics of the recruitment process. While Knowles (1980) lumps promotion and public relations together as part of his scheme for operating a comprehensive program, other authors distinguish between three terms: *public relations, marketing,* and *promotion.*

Public Relations. Activities undertaken to project a favorable image of a particular continuing education organization are referred to as *public relations.* These activities aim not at promoting acceptance of any one program but at establishing general awareness and positive attitudes toward both the sponsor and the range of services offered. The image should be visible to actual and prospective learners in everything the organization does (Knowles, 1980). Broadly construed, public relations precedes and underlies recruitment activities. Public relations relates "to the ability of the organizational unit to promote understanding and gain support from its own members and all those relevant others in other units of the larger organization as well as in external units" (Strother and Klus, 1982, p. 258). Public relations can be enhanced by what Knowles (1980) calls "building an educative climate within the organization" (p. 66), which is accomplished by providing a policy base, building an advisory committee structure, practicing a democratic philosophy, and exemplifying, as an organization, a propensity for change and growth.

Public relations strategies entail identifying the publics, planning the communications channels, conveying a message, and coordinating and evaluating the effort. Effective public relations can predispose target constituencies, including prospective adult students, to respond to specific programs that subsequent activities will promote. Low-cost public relations activities for a community-level continuing education organization include "piggyback ads, marquees, grocery bags, television identification slides, handouts at concerts, license plates on cars, book marks distributed at schools and libraries, feature articles in newspapers, tag lines in bill stuffers, and window displays in area businesses" (Ramsey, 1982, pp. 69–70).

Marketing. The term *marketing* refers to those steps in the program planning process designed to respond to the needs of specific target learners. Adapting a definition developed at Pitt Community College (1985), we can define marketing as the process of mapping the designated population within the sponsor's service area to determine its needs and wants and then fulfilling those needs and wants by developing a variety of specialized programs that will meet the educational needs of that and other segments of the prospective adult student population. The development of a marketing strategy has five steps: segmenting the market to be served, assessing the learning needs of target learners, setting precise objectives in accordance with those needs, promotion aimed at attracting target learners to appropriate programs, and guiding learners (Houle, 1972) into the learning activities. The authors of several chapters in this sourcebook treat each of these steps in varying degrees. This chapter considers only the second and fourth steps.

Once the overall population of prospective students has been mapped, the planners must decide which segments of that market are to be served. Recruitment efforts are often directed to the market segments that are easiest to identify and thus easiest to recruit: adults with relatively high levels of formal education and occupational status and ready access to discretionary financial, time, and other resources. While conventional marketing strategies may be adequate for these categories, conventional methods may be inadequate for adults who belong to such "excluded groups" as ethnic minority adults, low-income individuals, elderly senior citizens without families, the unemployed, displaced homemakers, immigrants, those who are not fluent in English, and undocumented workers.

Even within specific market segments, adults are not uniformly disposed to respond. In fact, by extending their marketing activities to a broad range of motivational orientations toward participation in sponsored learning, continuing educators may experience greater success in reducing the inhibitions of a larger percentage of prospective adult students and in increasing the likelihood of participation (Houle, 1985). Since Houle's (1961) pioneering study almost three decades ago, adult education theorists and researchers (Boshier, 1985a; Knoll, 1985) have elaborated on Houle's troika of motivational orientations—activity, goal, and learning. Nevertheless, few writers have examined the motivational orientations of those who do not participate in sponsored learning. It is therefore not surprising that the motivational orientations of current nonparticipants are not usually considered in segmenting the market for continuing education. Recognizing this omission, Houle (1985) expanded his original scheme to six categories: the oblivious person, the uninvolved person, the resistant person, the focused participant, the eclectic participant, and the comprehensive learner. Efforts aimed at segmenting the market should thus be directed not only to specific categories of prospective adult students but also to the wide range of motivational orientations toward sponsored learning manifest within those categories.

Promotion. Once the market segment has been identified, learning needs have been assessed, and specific program objectives have been set, the target students need to be induced to participate in the program.

Promotion is considered a subset of market activities. Drawing on diffusion theory, Rogers (1962) conceptualizes promotion as communication strategies aimed at guiding prospective students through the stages of awareness, interest, positive evaluation, and trial. To be effective, promotion must meet six criteria: First, the communication must reach the target group. Second, it must get their attention. Third, they must understand the message. Fourth, it must appeal to their needs. Fifth, it must persuade them that this is the preferred way of satisfying those needs. Sixth, it must be cost-effective (Strother and Klus, 1982).

The planning of promotional strategies involves a two-step process: first, identifying the channels of communication; second, designing the communications (Strother and Klus, 1982). The channels used can vary according to the designated categories or groups of target learners. For those most easy to influence, they include direct mail and newspaper, radio, and television ads. Less conventional ways, which have been shown to be effective with "excluded groups," include single-page leaflets; illustrated beer mats that can be distributed to pubs and clubs; feature articles in newspapers; radio and television spots; periodicals produced and edited by unemployed groups; publicity placed in community, drop-in, and job centers for the unemployed; displays in supermarkets and department stores; a traveling bus or mobile home; adult counseling services in community centers and public libraries; and door-to-door contacts (McDonald, 1984). Use of these less conventional channels represents a commitment to attract excluded adult students by capitalizing on specific social linkages or social support mechanisms via the organizations with which these adults affiliate (Schiamberg and Abler, 1986).

Obviously, recruitment strategies will vary with the nature, scope, and location both of the continuing education organization and of its parent organization. To sum up, the effectiveness of efforts to induce adult students to initiate volunteer participation in sponsored learning depends on the quality of the content and on the channels of information. Public relations enhances the proclivity of prospective learners to form favorable attitudes toward the program sponsor and the programs that it offers. Marketing activities permit the sponsor to accommodate prospective adult students with a range of motivational orientations from a variety of target markets. Promotion contributes to informed decisions on the part of adults to act on their dispositions to participate. Once the decision to participate has been made, the sponsor must turn its attention to the means whereby, via "motivation for continuance" (Boshier, 1985b, p. 134), that decision is upheld.

Retaining Adult Students

The retention of adult students reflects the capacity of the continuing education program to transform the student's initial commitment to participate into a commitment to continue that participation. Retention can also be regarded as the student's positive behavioral response to such distinctive features as the continuing education program, the organizational sponsor, and the learning experience itself.

The learner's motivational orientation and different aspects of the learners' life context external to the program also play a role. However, adult educators are limited in the extent to which they can affect these factors. Thus, adult educators are likely to find program and organizational features more amenable to modification. Such factors can be grouped into four categories: personal accommodation factors, instructional factors, governance factors, and program continuity factors.

Personal Accommodation Factors. Adults who participate in programs that have been tailored to their identified learning needs, that provide personal guidance—for example, personal and/or academic advising and preenrollment orientation—aimed at assuring them of the program's relevance to their current life situation, that provide access to financial resources when necessary, that provide some means of interpreting the experience to employers or others with whom the learners are associated, and that have been scheduled at convenient times and places are likely to feel more comfortable about their learning activities than adults in programs that do not meet these criteria.

Instructional Factors. Because the instructor in the continuing education program can interact affectively with students and develop particularistic relations with students, different aspects of the instructional setting can have more influence on the nature and rate of retention of adult students than the overall continuing education organization, which usually operates more on the basis of universalistic criteria and affective neutrality (Bidwell, 1965). Where students find a close correspondence between instructional objectives and their own learning objectives, find that learning tasks are moderately difficult and challenging, recognize the relevance of what is being learned, experience success as mastery of the knowledge and skills, are favorably disposed toward the ways in which instruction is carried out, perceive the instructor to be both competent and supportive (Beaudin, 1982), and relate well to instructors in the program, they are more likely to continue their participation. In the event that instructors, instruction, and instructional materials are deficient, the adult educator may need to institute staff development, modify the program, or both.

Another aspect of the instructional setting that has an effect on retention is the learning group experience (Jensen, 1964). From group dynamics research, we know that a group's shared perceptions can influence the perceptions of individual members. Thus, the academic achievement of the group as a whole, the sense of group cohesiveness, the degree to which all group members take an active part, the positive evaluation of the shared experience, and the learning success of individual group members are all operational indicators of a successful continuing education program. As such, they point to the importance of the social interaction dimension of participation in continuing education. They also reflect important components of the capacity of the program to retain students.

Governance Factors. The third factor in retention relates to the participatory and power-sharing element of the overall program. People who are active in the decision-making processes of the institution are more likely to form an ongoing commitment to the institution. Adult educators who foster active advisory committees not only make assessments of learning needs more effective but also signal to prospective learners that they are committed to making the program personally relevant to learners. Likewise, educators can build structures for the reception and processing of feedback from participants into their programs as formative, summative, and impact evaluations. Participating adult students can be invited to collaborate with instructors and administrators in instructional and program planning. Such collaboration gives them opportunities to identify with and develop a sense of loyalty to the program. Their program becomes "our" program.

Program Continuity Factors. The fourth factor in retention involves the retention capacity that can be transferred from one program to another. When programs comprise elements of a meaningful set of programs—for example, when a certain number of courses comprises a baccalaureate of liberal studies—the retention capacity for the overall set may exceed the retention capacity for any one course. Program continuity factors signal to instructors and others in the organization that corrective action is needed when a student encounters difficulty that, without resolution, may cause the student to drop out.

Summary

In continuing education, recruitment is the step in program planning whereby adults are inducted into a program of systematic learning. Recruitment can be conceptualized as a function of public relations, marketing, and promotion activities that the continuing education organization carries out in support of its continuing education programs. Promotion activities should be geared to the full range of prospective adult students, not just to those predisposed to participate in a given program.

Retention in continuing education relates to the capacity of the program to transform the initial commitment of adult students into continuing participation. An overall strategy to increase retention will take at least four sets of program retention factors into account: personal accommodation factors, instructional factors, governance factors, and program continuity factors.

Recruitment and retention are interrelated activities. Ideally, both program promotion and marketing activities should focus on and highlight those aspects of the program that are anticipated to be most conducive to student retention. Adult students are more likely both to initiate participation and to continue participation when recruitment and retention activities are congruent.

References

Beaudin, B. *Retaining Adult Students. Overview.* ERIC Fact Sheet No. 12. Columbus, Ohio: ERIC Clearinghouse on Adult, Career, and Vocational Education, 1982. (ED 237 800)
Bidwell, C. E. "The School as a Formal Organization." In J. B. March (ed.), *Handbook of Organizations.* Chicago: Rand McNally, 1965.
Boshier, R. "Adult Education: Motivation of Participants." In T. Husen and T. N. Postlewaite (eds.), *The International Encyclopedia of Education.* Oxford: Pergamon Press, 1985a.
Boshier, R. "Motivation for Adult Education: A Summary of Discussions." In J. H. Knoll (ed.), *Motivation for Adult Education.* Bonn: German Commission for UNESCO, 1985b.
Darkenwald, G. G. *Retaining Adult Students.* Columbus, Ohio: ERIC Clearinghouse on Adult, Career, and Vocational Education, 1981.
Darkenwald, G. G. "Keep Your ADA." In C. Klevins (ed.), *Materials and Methods in Adult and Continuing Education.* Los Angeles: Klevens, 1982.
Houle, C. O. *The Inquiring Mind.* Madison: University of Wisconsin Press, 1961.
Houle, C. O. *The Design of Education.* San Francisco: Jossey-Bass, 1972.
Houle, C. O. "Structural Features and Policies Promoting (or Inhibiting) Adult Learners." In J. H. Knoll (ed.), *Motivation for Adult Education.* Bonn: German Commission for UNESCO, 1985.
Jensen, G. "Social Psychology and Adult Education Practice." In G. Jensen, A. A. Liveright, and W. Hallenbeck (eds.), *Adult Education: Outlines of an Emerging Field of University Study.* Washington, D.C.: Adult Education Association of the U.S.A., 1964.
Knoll, J. H. (ed.). *Motivation for Adult Education.* Bonn.: German Commission for UNESCO, 1985.
Knowles, M. S. *The Modern Practice of Adult Education: From Pedagogy to Andragogy.* Chicago: Follett, 1980.
McDonald, J. *Education for Unemployed Adults: Problems and Good Practice. REPLAN Report.* London: Department of Education and Science, 1984. (ED 259 116)
Pitt Community College. *A Model for Recruiting the New Community College Student.* Greenville, N.C.: Pitt Community College, 1985. (ED 267 187)
Ramsey, D. "Making the Most of Free Promotions." In R. V. Conter and W. A. Porcelli (eds.), *Removing Barriers to the Adult Learner Through Marketing, Management, and Programming: Proceedings of the NUCEA Region VI Conference.* Tucson: University of Arizona Continuing Education, 1982. (ED 227 247)
Rogers, E. M. *Diffusion of Innovations.* New York: Free Press, 1962.

Schiamberg, L. B., and Abler, W. "The Ecology of Social Support and Older Adult Adaptation: A Review of Research and Educational Implications." Paper presented at the annual meeting of the American Educational Research Association, San Francisco, 1986. (ED 275 836)

Strother, G. B., and Klus, J. P. *Administration of Continuing Education.* Belmont, Calif.: Wadsworth, 1982.

Peter S. Cookson is associate professor of adult education and professor-in-charge of the Adult Education Program at Pennsylvania State University.

Two examples of organizational theory provide a framework within which the organizational tasks required to initiate and maintain continuing education programs can be conceptualized.

Recruiting and Retaining Adult Students: An Organizational Theory Perspective

Peter S. Cookson

Surveys in the U.S. have reported rates of participation in formally organized adult education programs to be around 30 percent (Carp, Peterson, and Roelfs, 1974). The literature on participation in continuing education places the primary emphasis on the psychological characteristics of adult learners. This emphasis has obscured the role of organizations in the provision of adult education, which is enormously significant. A vast body of knowledge that can provide a framework for organizational functioning lies waiting to be tapped by adult educators.

Kast and Rosenzweig (1974, p. 9) define organizational theory as "the body of knowledge, including hypotheses and propositions, stemming from . . . *organization science*." Organizational theorists draw from the behavioral and social sciences to "understand the increasingly complex nature of organizations in a dynamic environment and the attendant difficult problem-solving task of managers" (Kast and Rosenzweig, 1974, p. 19). Organization theory that withstands the tests of rigorous empirical research using scientific methods can provide guidelines for management (Kast and Rosenzweig, 1974).

This chapter describes the recruitment and retention of adult students in light of two varieties of organizational theory. The first, termed *compliance theory*, was formulated by Etzioni (1961, 1975) to classify the relationships between organizational representatives and "lower participants" in large organizations. The second is open-systems theory as interpreted by Kast and Rosenzweig (1974) and Katz and Kahn (1978). I will describe each theory and illustrate it with examples drawn from various continuing education situations.

Compliance Theory

Compliance theory drives from a proposal by Etzioni (1975) to differentiate organizations on the basis of power and control. Etzioni (1975, p. 4) defines power as "an actor's ability to induce or influence another actor to carry out his directives or any other norms he supports." The fundamental question, according to Pugh, Hickson, and Hinings (1971, p. 20) is, "Why do people in organizations conform to the orders given to them and follow the standards of behavior laid down for them?" For continuing education, the question is, Why do people choose to participate in a continuing education program, and, once they have begun, why do they choose to continue in that program? To answer these questions, Etzioni (1975) proposes comparative studies of both structure and motivational patterns within different types of organizations.

The core variable in Etzioni's scheme is *compliance,* "a relationship consisting of the power employed by superiors to control subordinates and the orientation of the subordinate to this power" (Etzioni, 1975, p. xv). Organizations can be classified according to the form of power applied to "lower participants" that dominates as coercive, remunerative, or normative, and involvement can be classified as alienative, calculative, or moral.

Although there are nine possible combinations of power and involvement, one form of involvement is "congruent" with each form of power. The other combinations are incongruent and inherently unstable. For members of organizations that exercise coercive power, which rests on the use of physical force, restriction of activities, and restraint, the dominant reaction is alienation, and the resulting compliance is coercive. For members of organizations that exercise remunerative power, which emphasizes control over material resources, distribution of wages, and allocation of fringe benefits, the dominant reaction is calculative involvement, and the resulting compliance is utilitarian. For members of organizations that exercise normative power, which manages the "allocation and manipulation of symbolic rewards and deprivations through the employment of leaders, manipulation of mass media, allocation of esteem and prestige symbols" (Etzioni, 1961, p. 5), the dominant reaction is moral involvement, and the resulting compliance is normative (Etzioni, 1975). These relations between power and involvement are evident in organizations as a whole and within their subunits.

Applied to continuing education, Etzioni's scheme enables us to predict the kinds of relations that are most likely to occur. Prospective adult students may be pressured to attend a continuing education program under threat of loss of third-party-assigned benefits or privileges. For example, in some states, prison inmates who lack literacy or job skills have been given an ultimatum either of engaging in prison education or of prolonging their sentence. Welfare recipients have been sometimes required to participate in job skills training or else lose their monthly allotment. Although recruitment and retention can and do occur under coercive conditions, the resulting alienation can exact a high price in terms of ineffectual learning. If the attention of these students could be directed away from the benefits or privileges that they may lose toward the benefits and privileges that they stand to gain from participation, their compliance would perhaps become less alienative and more calculative. Nevertheless, the change would be as inherently unstable as it was unlikely, since the organization's actual goals would thus be incongruent with its compliance structure (Etzioni, 1975).

For an example of a continuing education program with a predominantly remunerative power orientation, we can look to an industrial training program in which participants receive compensation for attendance. The motivation of these participants is calculative; that is, they participate for reasons extraneous to the learning tasks, not out of a desire to learn. As long as the sponsoring organization is prepared to allocate resources aimed at prompting recruitment and retention, participants can be expected to respond. A pattern of remunerative-calculative relations may thus be established. Such relations, characterized by manipulation of pay, fines, and bonuses, seldom lead to the internalization of values. At best, they produce superficial, expedient, overt commitment (Etzioni, 1975). Thus, if the resources with which the sponsor compensates participants are exhausted, recruitment and retention rates are likely to drop. Such has been the experience with adult students, whether they were low-income adults in American inner cities or cottage entrepreneurs in rural Bangladesh who, after years of being paid to attend educational programs, will not now attend a program in the absence of financial compensation.

Like other educative institutions, continuing education organizations are culture oriented, specializing as they do in the reproduction or transfer of the cultural heritage and in the creation of new culture. Normative-moral relations are characterized by high commitment on the part of participants, who attend not out of a sense of obligation or extrinsic reward but rather out of a sense of duty or pleasure. Etzioni (1975, p. 6) explains the two kinds of normative power: "One is based on the manipulation of esteem, prestige, and ritualistic symbols [such as credits, certificates, degrees]; the other, on allocation and manipulation of acceptance and positive response." The first kind of normative power is typical of the factors germane to the recruitment efforts of the sponsoring organization. According to Carp, Peterson, and Roelfs (1974, p. 42), the most significant reason for which adults respond to the recruitment efforts of adult educators is to become better informed. The second kind of normative power is more typical of the social influence inherent in the instructional and other factors impinging on retention of adult students.

One drawback of compliance theory is that it depends on a single dimension of organizational functioning and overlooks other aspects of organizations. Open-systems theory offers a more comprehensive overview of organizational functioning.

Open-Systems Theory

The concept of *system* underlies many organizational theories. The concept of system suggests that the organization should be viewed as a unitary whole and as a dynamic relationship between that whole and its interdependent parts or subsystems on the one hand and its environmental suprasystem on the other. The concept of system may also refer to organizational processes that include inputs, throughputs, and outputs. *Open-systems theory* emphasizes the nature of the interaction between an organization and its environment whereby the organization receives essential energy and other resources required for survival. Katz and Kahn (1978) list the ten characteristics of open systems. These characteristics have meaning not only for programs sponsored by continuing education organizations but also for the recruitment and retention of adult students.

Importation of Energy. Organizations must obtain resources from their environment in order to survive and thrive. Production inputs consist of "materials and energies directly related to the throughput, the work that comprises the activity of the organization in turning out a product" (Katz and Kahn, 1978, p. 754). For continuing education, organization energy is derived from the recommendations of advisory committees, program plans, instructional technology and devices, people who become students, income generated to pay for the educational programs, materials and people related to program delivery, and exchange of resources with collaborating organizations. Maintenance inputs consist of "the energetic and informational contributions necessary to hold the people in the system and persuade them to carry out their activities as members of the system" (Katz and Kahn, 1978, p. 754). For continuing education organizations, the communications that guide adult learners into the program, instructional objectives and interactions, the congruence between instructional situation and individual goals and objectives, the patterns of social reinforcement, governance policies, and any coupling between the current program and antecedent and subsequent programs are not only maintenance inputs but factors that enhance the retention of adult students.

Throughput. As "input processors" (Jackson, Morgan, and Paolillo, 1986, p. 13), organizations transform the raw inputs into products or services that the external environment can use. First, the process of recruitment transforms prospective adult participants into actual adult students. Financial resources derived from registration fees and other income are converted into material and human resources to be utilized in the process of instruction. Retention is enhanced as adult students engage in satisfying and nurturing learning experiences and in supportive social relations with their instructors and peers.

Output. The inputs that the organization processes are eventually exported to the environment. If the transformation process in a continuing education program is effective, the outputs include learning achievement, satisfaction with the experience, group cohesiveness, and the formation of a commitment to such activities in the future. If the actual program outputs meet the needs and expectations of the adult students, retention can be expected to be high, and the program can be expected to continue.

Systems as Cycles of Events. The input-throughput-output cycle can be expected to continue as long as the organization works effectively and efficiently. Knowledge that students tend to obtain the knowledge and skills that they desired at the time of recruitment tends to enhance further recruitment efforts.

Negative Entropy. The law of entropy suggests that all organizations tend to move toward disorganization and demise (Jackson, Morgan, and Paolillo, 1986). Steps must be taken to prevent such an eventuality. Negative entropy is accomplished by *storing* surplus or excess energy imported from the environment as funds, credit, or organizational *slack* that can be used later in the event that there is a deficit of energy. Continuing education organizations commonly operate according to the *Robin Hood principle* whereby the excess "spread" from certain profitable programs is placed in reserve, where it can be drawn on to support programs that operate at a loss.

Information Input. Besides energy information concerning relevant aspects of the environment constitutes significant input because it allows the organization to accommodate changing aspects of the external environment. The marketing process permits the flow of communication between the organization and the environment about critical elements of the organization's products and services on the one hand and the learning needs of individuals and organizations that those products and services should address on the other.

The Steady State. Although elements both internal and external to the organization preclude the attainment of homeostasis, an organization that arrests entropy by attaining a measure of control over its environment can reach a steady state. A continuing education organization that has reliable sources of new recruits and that provides reliable and valued services can operate continuing education programs at a predictably constant level. Effective recruitment and retention strategies assure maintenance of this steady state.

Differentiation. In response to conditions within their environments, evolving organizations become more specialized and differentiated in the outputs that they export to the environment. When a continuing education organization that has been offering successful programming for certain kinds of adults decides to broaden its recruitment efforts in order to attract other groups, it begins to grow and expand. To increase the effectiveness of recruitment and retention activities, marketing and program specialists are hired. Adult student markets may become more segmented. New staff members who specialize in delivery to certain categories of target learners can begin to supplement the work of more generalist staff members. The volume of throughputs increases in response to the increased flow of inputs. Certain programs are modified so as to appeal to other types of adult learners.

Integration and Coordination. As differentiation and specialization increase, so does the need to reintegrate diverse organizational activities. Enhanced integration and coordination activities can include "control mechanisms, priority setting, rules, meetings, standard operating procedures, and scheduling" (Jackson, Morgan, and Paolillo, 1986, p. 15). A continuing education organization can hire an assistant director to assume many of the director's day-to-day administrative tasks so the director can devote more energy to overall coordination and planning. New staff members can be hired to coordinate activities at outreach sites where the number of separate programs is increasing.

Equifinality. The tendency of open systems to use a variety of different routes to attain their objectives is referred to as *equifinality*. Continuing education organizations can use a wide variety of strategies to recruit and retain adult students. Depending both on the particular program being offered and on other factors, mass-media advertising can attract as many adult students to a program viewed as successful as referrals and word of mouth.

Open-Systems Theory and Organizational Subsystems

Since adult students must be attracted from the environment, educators can use the characteristics of open systems just enumerated to examine the relations between their own organization and its external environment. Adult educators can use an open-systems frame of reference to determine why recruitment or retention results may have slumped in their own situation or to justify actions designed to increase the productivity of recruitment and retention efforts.

Additional insights can be gained from the contributions of the systems approach to organizational structure. Viewed as a system, an organization is defined as a subsystem of a suprasystem—the organization's broader environment—that, guided by goals and values, coordinates the activities of a technical subsystem, a structural subsystem, a psychosocial subsystem, and a managerial subsystem (Kast and Rosenzweig, 1974).

Each of these elements deserves further comment. The *suprasystem* is differentiated from the organization by permeable boundaries. The other five elements correspond to the organization's five subsystems.

The Goals and Values Subsystem. The suprasystem often determines the organization's reason for being as well as its goals and values. For example, continuing education organizations exist to enable men and women to engage in purposeful and systematic learning. They may also exist to increase the effectiveness, efficiency, profitability, and credibility of the parent organization. While the goals and values of the continuing education organization may be declared in the organization's charter or mission statement, the goals and values that are pursued in practice comprise the goals and values subsystem. In this regard, there is no clearer evidence of the goals and values of a continuing education organization than in its record of recruitment and retention of adult students.

The Technical Subsystem. The specialized knowledge and skills that an organization requires in order to transform inputs from the environment into throughputs that it exports to the environment comprise the technical subsystem. Organizations with more efficient technical subsystems can be expected to demonstrate higher levels of exchange than organizations with less efficient technical subsystems. Accordingly, continuing education organizations whose staff members and resources match the learning needs of targeted audiences of adult learners are more likely to report higher levels of recruitment and retention than organizations that are not so well endowed. Likewise, a continuing education organization that commands the resources for sophisticated marketing strategies is better able to pinpoint specific market segments and thus increase the likelihood of specialized programs than organizations that do not.

The Structural Subsystem. The structural subsystem consists of the ways in which the work of the organization gets done. These ways include the assignment of roles and relationships—how tasks are divided among individuals who occupy different positions (differentiation) and how they are coordinated by upper management (integration). As Kast and Rosenzweig (1974, p. 112) explain, "In the formal sense, structure is set forth by the organization charts, by position and job descriptions, and by rules and procedures. It is also concerned with patterns of authority, communication, and work flow." If recruitment and retention of adult students are to take place effectively and efficiently, these functions will need not only to be clearly defined within the structural subsystem but also to be structured so as to accommodate the particular life-styles of prospective adult students.

The Psychosocial Subsystem. An organization consists of interacting individuals and groups. "It consists of individual behavior and motivation, status and role relationships, group dynamics, and influence systems. It is also affected by sentiments, values, attitudes, expectations, and aspirations of the people in the organization" (Kast and Rosenzweig, 1974, p. 111). For recruitment and retention practices in continuing education, the nature of the interaction between continuing education administrators and instructors and program participants can have a significant impact on program outcomes. If organizational representatives are sensitive and sympathetic to the organization's goals and values, they are more likely to evoke what Knowles (1980, p. 66) calls an "educative environment for learning," and adult students are more likely to respond to the organization's recruitment and retention efforts in positive ways.

The Managerial Subsystem. The major task of the manager is to coordinate and integrate the other four subsystems and the environmental suprasystem. Managerial tasks can be subdivided into strategic, coordinative, and operating dimensions or levels as the organization relates to the environmental suprasystem and the four subsystems. Within a continuing education organization, counselors, advisers, programmers, media specialists, instructors, and students are found at the operating level. Advisory committees, outside consultants, higher-level administrators in the parent organization, professional association officers, and government policymakers are found at the strategic level. From the systems perspective, the role of the manager is to bring the management focuses of planning, organizing, and controlling into play and thus to unify the efforts of the lower and higher levels within the organization. The challenge is to translate the long-range and more general perspectives of actors at the strategic level into specific objectives and activities for actors at the operating level. With regard to the recruitment and retention of adult students, the continuing educator must be supportive of recruitment and retention practices at each of these three levels. At the strategic level, policies and procedures aimed at attracting adult students to educational programs and at encouraging them to persist in their attendance need to be established. At the operational level, those who have interpersonal contact with adult students need to deliver educational services in effective and nurturing ways. At the coordinative level, the policies of the strategic level need to be juxtapositioned with the working requirements of the operational level. Because environments are constantly in flux, the continuing education manager must make sure that the organization's subsystems are adaptive, that they match the dynamic of the suprasystem, and that the boundaries between the organization and its environments remain permeable.

Significance of Organizational Theory for Recruiting and Retaining Adult Students

What do compliance theory and open-systems theory add to our understanding of how adult educators can improve their organization's efforts to recruit and retain adult students?

Compliance theory draws attention to the nature of the power or control that organizations exercise in relation to "lower participants." The key is to achieve a consonance or balance between the type of power exercised within the organization and the type of involvement expected of those who elect to participate in activities sponsored by the organization. If persistent participation is deemed desirable, then the organization must foster either calculative or moral involvement. Each outcome calls for divergent control strategies on the part of the organization. Even in organizations in which calculative or coercive control relations prevail, movement toward the normative-moral involvement is desirable.

Open-systems theory calls attention to the interrelatedness of processes and structures internal to the organization and to the exchange between those subsystems and the environmental suprasystem external to the organization. The managerial subsystem coordinates and integrates all subsystems and maintains permeable boundaries among the subsystems and between them and the environment. Changes in the environment can have pronounced implications for recruitment and retention practices. Unless the subsystems are informed of and able to respond to such changes, recruitment and retention can suffer.

The importance of organizational responsiveness to the changes in the suprasystem was reported to me in an interview a numbers of years ago by the director of the Sacramento (California) City College Continuing Education Program who foresaw the need to replace mechanical typewriters and calculators with electronic machines. Forewarned by the program's advisory committee, he alerted the technical and structural subsystems of his organization—at least those responsible for courses and certification programs relating to office machine maintenance and repair—and coordinated a modernization process. Instructors received advanced training from the manufacturers of the new electronic equipment. Because his organization was the first in its service area to update, the continuing education program captured all members of a particular group of adult students in the community. As a result, several proprietary schools suddenly found themselves unable to compete and subsequently phased out a line of once prosperous programs.

Awareness of open-systems theory can thus make adult educators aware of the importance and necessity of adapting and responding to the organization's environment, which is where prospective adult students are to be found. Continuing educators sensitive to their leadership role can ensure that the managerial subsystem effectively coordinates the work of other organization subsystems in presenting unified policies and procedures for the successful recruitment and retention of adult students.

References

Carp, A., Peterson, R., and Roelfs, P. "Adult Learning Interests and Experiences." In K. P. Cross, J. R. Valley, and Associates, *Planning Non-Traditional Programs: An Analysis of the Issues for Postsecondary Education.* San Francisco: Jossey-Bass, 1974.

Etzioni, A. *The Comparative Analysis of Complex Organizations.* New York: Free Press, 1961.

Etzioni, A. *The Comparative Analysis of Complex Organizations.* (2nd ed.) New York: Free Press, 1975.

Jackson, J. H., Morgan, C. P., and Paolillo, J.G.P. *Organization Theory: A Macro Perspective for Management.* Englewood Cliffs, N.J.: Prentice-Hall, 1986.

Kast, F. E., and Rosenzweig, J. E. *Organization and Management: A Systems Approach.* (2nd ed.) New York: McGraw-Hill, 1974.

Katz, D., and Kahn, R. L. *The Social Psychology of Organizing.* (2nd ed.) New York: Wiley, 1978.

Knowles, M. S. *The Modern Practice of Adult Education: From Pedagogy to Andragogy.* Chicago: Follett, 1980.

Pugh, D. S., Hickson, D. J., and Hinings, C. R. *Writers on Organizations.* Harmondsworth, England: Penguin, 1971.

Peter S. Cookson is associate professor of adult education and professor-in-charge of the Adult Education Program at Pennsylvania State University.

The recruitment and the retention of adults in educational programs are influenced by a program planning perspective that resembles modern marketing.

Recruiting and Retaining Adult Students: A Marketing Perspective

William S. Griffith

No adult education program can reasonably be regarded as effective unless it is successful both in recruiting an adequate number of participants from a previously defined target audience and in keeping those participants actively involved in the program until it has been completed. Whether the program is fully self-supporting from student fees or entirely subsidized, it can scarcely be considered to have achieved its purposes if it cannot attract the desired students or maintain the interest of those who have been attracted for the duration of the program. In the case of the self-supporting program that gets all its income from the fees paid by participants, the program cannot be conducted unless an adequate number of students have been persuaded to enroll and pay the registration fee. In fact, it cannot run even once unless additional funds can be secured from another source to cover the costs. If program planners are successful in attracting an audience for the first offering of a program but registrants drop out before they complete it, the planners will have difficulty attracting another group of paying customers for a second offering of the same program. Accordingly, whether the institutional provider uses third-party funding or the participants themselves pay all or part of the costs of the program, both recruitment and retention are fundamental processes that each program planner must consider if successful programs are to be developed. This chapter considers the application of a marketing perspective to the planning and operation of adult education programs.

Marketing and Program Planning

Although marketing has not traditionally been included in adult education program planning models, it seems reasonable to regard marketing as a logical part of the program planning process. This chapter relates the elements of program planning to the range of factors that various authors have identified as parts of the marketing strategy.

Beder (1986) stresses that sound marketing depends on clarity of mission. Without such clarity, he believes, programs will lack coherence, and that affects rates of participation. Falk (1986, pp. 49-50), who regards marketing as promotion, states that "The function of promotion in continuing education is to present accurate and persuasive messages to prospective students or clients and to stimulate interest in particular offerings or services." The ethical marketer is also the ethical program planner, who seeks to design programs that meet the specific needs of particular target groups, then attempts to inform the intended audience about the program so that the desired participation occurs.

Kotler (1975), who has written what is probably the best-known book on marketing for nonprofit organizations, defines marketing as "the effective management by an organization of its exchange relations with its various markets and publics. . . . Marketing is the organization's undertaking of analysis, planning, implementation, and control to achieve its exchange objectives with its target markets" (Kotler, 1975, p. x). In Kotler's (1975) view, marketing encompasses functions that authors in adult education consider to be part of the program planning process.

Kotler (1975, p. 9) asserts that "Organizations in a free society depend upon voluntary exchanges to accomplish their objectives. Resources must be attracted, employees must be stimulated, customers must be found. The designing of proper incentives is a key step in stimulating these exchanges. Marketing is the applied science most concerned with managing exchanges effectively and efficiently."

Marketing Orientations. From a marketing perspective, Kotler (1975) classifies organizations into four types: Unresponsive organizations do nothing to measure the needs, perceptions, preferences, or satisfactions of their constituent publics. Casually responsive organizations show an interest in learning about customer needs, perceptions, preferences, and satisfactions. Highly responsive organizations show a keen interest in learning about the needs, perceptions, preferences, and satisfactions of their constituents and rely on systematic information collection procedures, such as formal opinion surveys and consumer panels. Fully responsive organizations formally audit at regular intervals the needs, perceptions, preferences, and satisfactions of their constituent publics, which they encourage to participate actively in the affairs of the organization and to vent their complaints, suggestions, and opinions through formal and informal systems. Most organizations, agencies, and associations active in adult education would probably fall into the third group, although they would probably express a desire to operate like organizations in the fourth group.

Kotler (1975) notes that, while organizations normally start out with a clear purpose to serve some class of human needs, they add new activities over time and become inwardly oriented. In such cases, the organization becomes increasingly unresponsive to emerging needs and trends.

Marketing Audits. If an organization becomes sufficiently concerned about its ability to carry out its functions effectively and efficiently, Kotler (1975) suggests that the organization should conduct a marketing audit. He defines *marketing audit* as an independent examination of the entire marketing effort of an organization that covers objectives, programs, implementation, organizations, and control. The purpose of an audit is to determine what is being done and to recommend what should be done in the future. A marketing audit is conducted in three parts: The first part evaluates the organization's marketing environment—its markets, customers, competitors, and macroenvironment. The second part evaluates the marketing system within the organization—the organization's objectives, programs, implementation, and organization. The third part evaluates the major areas of marketing activity in the organization—its products, pricing, distribution, personal contact, advertising, publicity, and sales promotion.

A Classification of Demand. Kotler (1975) identifies three main categories of demand: underdemand, adequate demand, and overdemand. Within the category of underdemand, he distinguishes negative demand (all or most important segments of the market are uninterested in or indifferent to a particular offering), latent demand (all or most important segments of the market share a strong need for something that does not exist currently), and faltering demand (demand for the product has slowed, and further decline is anticipated). Within the category of adequate demand, he distinguishes irregular demand (the pattern of demand is marked by seasonal or volatile changes) from full demand (both the level and the timing of demand are equal to the desired level and timing). Last, within the category of overdemand, he differentiates between overfull demand (demand for the product exceeds the level at which the marketer feels able or motivated to supply it) and unwholesome demand (any positive level of demand is felt to be excessive because of the unde sirable qualities associated with offering it). Underdemand poses a greater problem for adult educators than overdemand.

Market Definition and Segmentation. The process in which an organization analyzes the market for a product that it offers is called *market definition*. During this process, the public is divided into at least three groups: the actual market, composed of those who are already interested in the product; the potential market, composed of those who may become interested in the product; and the nonmarket, composed of those will never become interested in the product. The step of dividing the market into fairly homogeneous parts according to the predicted responses of its members is called *market segmentation*.

The information acquired in defining the market enables the organization to choose the type of marketing mix that it wishes to use. In undifferentiated marketing, the organization chooses to treat the whole market as homogeneous, focusing on what is common to all members of the market, not on what is different; in this case no market segmentation is involved. In concentrated marketing, the organization decides to divide the market into meaningful segments and devote its efforts to a single segment. In differentiated marketing, the organization decides to focus on two or more segments of the market; in this case, a separate marketing program is devised for each segment.

Falk (1986, p. 54) maintains that "The major challenge in making decisions about promotion is to ensure to the greatest practical extent that the persons for whom programs are intended will receive information in a timely manner." Adult education has made little effort to develop market segmentation. As a result, most publicity about adult education is disseminated in a shotgun manner. However, some creative programmers have adopted concentrated and even differentiated marketing. Since exchange is the central concept underlying marketing, Buckmaster (1985) argues that information—both about the intended audience and about the programs and plans of competitors—is the essential ingredient. She advocates the establishment of a systematic approach to information gathering through such internal sources as program faculty, employees, and students and through such external sources as mail surveys, personal interviews, sampling, and focus groups. Program planners can use the resulting information to determine market populations and their needs, create programs that meet those needs, and thus promote programs to specific target populations. The net result of this activity should be an increase in the recruitment of adult learners.

Stern (1983, p. 9), administrator of the extension program of the University of California at Berkeley and longtime observer of the evolution of continuing professional education, has observed: "Because of the billions of dollars involved, because of its importance as part of our gross national product, because maintenance of professional competence is crucial to the ultimate consumer, [continuing professional education] must be viewed not only from the philosophic or educational point of view but politically and economically as a market, or, more precisely, as markets." The number of regulatory groups authorized to exert control over the marketing of continuing professional education is growing. Other segments of the adult education market may soon be facing increasing controls as governments seek to protect the public interest. Governments exert some control over marketing. Insofar as education is regarded as a commercial activity, such control may be one of the appropriate constraints on advertising.

Defining Needs. According to Kotler (1975), the concept of needs presents three operational problems. First, there is no clear definition of need that would enable an objective assessment of conditions to be made. Instead, the term is used interchangeably with *want, desire,* and *demand*—a situation that does not lead to clarification. Second, people have usually not given their needs any sustained thought. Even if they have, they commonly experience great difficulty in expressing them clearly, or they may be reluctant to discuss them. In any event, it is difficult to extract the public's perceptions in an objective and valid manner. Third, even when a number of needs have been identified, estimating the relative importance or intensity of the needs is a complex problem. Accordingly, the process of needs assessment is far from sound and objective. Effective marketing requires a systematic approach to needs assessment if concentrated or differentiated marketing is to be achieved.

Reconceptualizing the Adult Education Product. Kotler (1975) stresses that it is useful to conceptualize the product in three ways: First, the tangible product is the physical entity or service that is offered to the target market. Second, the core product is the essential utility or benefit that the buyer perceives in the product. Third, the augmented product is the totality of the costs and benefits that the buyer experiences or receives upon acquiring the product. Adult education programmers have tended to emphasize the tangible product and to leave any consideration of the core product to the potential participants.

Beder (1986) has differentiated between the instrumental and expressive benefits of participation in education products. The instrumental benefits are those that serve as a means to some other desired end. The expressive benefits are the feelings of pleasure or gratification that result from the act of participation itself or from the learning acquired through participation. In either case, the efforts that the program planner invests in identifying both the instrumental and the expressive benefits from each program can lead to increased enrollment.

Problem Analysis. Kotler (1975), who presents several case studies of marketing problems, uses the case of unmotivated students. Although he does not analyze the problem in detail, his preliminary analysis leads him to conclude the following: The problem of unmotivated students requires educators to identify the reasons for undermotivation. Do they lie in the product? the teaching methods? the school atmosphere? By altering the product, by offering alternative products, or by changing incentives, the institution might be able to improve students' views of the product. It seems clear that the astute marketer addresses many of the same concerns as an insightful program planner.

Planning with a Marketing Perspective

The recruiting process, which can be viewed as part of the marketing strategy, involves several elements from traditional program planning models. In outlining the elements to be considered when a suitable format for an adult education program is designed, Houle (1972) lists resources, leaders, methods, schedule, social reinforcement, roles and relationships, clarity of design, the life-style of the intended audience, finance, and interpretation and guidance. A marketing plan must consider each of these elements.

Choosing Resources. The choice of resources, including the venue for the activity, can increase or diminish the appeal of any program. Information about the meeting place and the facilities there can serve to attract those members of the target audience who have some concern about such matters. Mason (1986, p. 86) maintains that "Location is the key to success when programs are designed for military personnel, prison inmates, or professionals who desire to combine a vacation in a desired location with a continuing education activity. . . . The image, or symbolic value, of an off-campus location may be of major concern in some cases . . . the choice of location should be related to specific goals of the continuing education unit."

Selecting Leaders. Leaders are often selected for their established reputations because they will enhance the appeal of a program. The marketing process simply makes known the quality of the leaders. Potential participants can use that information in determining whether to take part in the program.

Describing the Format. Advance announcements of the program's formats—lectures, field trips, film viewing, discussion groups, to name only some of the possibilities—can help potential participants to assess the match between the program and their own interests and preferences. If potential participants are well informed about the methods to be employed, they will not be surprised or disappointed after they have enrolled.

Social Reinforcement. The matter of social reinforcement is of interest to at least some members of the target audience. Knowledge of any social events built into the program will help possible participants to decide whether they want to invest time and effort in the learning activity. The emotional aspects of interpersonal relationships are important within groups of learners, so it is important for participants to be able to anticipate the sort of social environment that will prevail.

Roles and Relationships. Roles and relationships matter to prospective learners in the degree that the nature of the other participants affects their freedom to interact. Situations that threaten an individual's status are not conducive to harmonious learning. Potential participants like to be informed about the probable nature of the learning group and the roles that the leaders and the adult students are expected to play. Timely information makes it possible for individuals to avoid learning activities in settings that might be likely to be unpleasant or threatening.

Explaining the Design. In some cases, planners do an excellent job of arranging a schedule and choosing leaders for an educational activity, but they do not spend the additional time required to explain to potential participants exactly what is expected of them and how their time at the activity will be spent. Every potential recruit is entitled to a schedule that makes clear what is going to be happening at each part of the program and what sort of involvement the individual participant is expected to have. Without adequate knowledge of the program design, those who enroll may withdraw when the unfolding program violates their expectations.

Recruiting the Right Audience. In an effort to recruit an audience that is sufficiently large to make a program both educationally and financially profitable, planners may neglect to inform potential participants about the prior training and background that those who take part in the program should have. Full information concerning the leader's assumptions about the audience's background and experience enables individuals to make informed decisions that prevent them from registering for programs for which they are inadequately prepared. Guiding adults away from programs that are not suitable for them is one part of the larger task of programming for specific segments of the public. It is also an important consideration in ethical marketing.

Life-Style Considerations. Planners cannot afford not to consider the life-styles of the potential participants. In some communities, it would be unwise to plan any education activities outside churches on Sunday mornings. In other communities, families may well use this time to engage in outings. Income levels, eating habits, traveling preferences, and other socioeconomic variables can all influence the appeal of the programs offered by adult educators. Adult educators are well advised to learn a great deal about the life-styles of their potential audiences so as not to plan activities that violate established ways of living and cause the intended learners to become resistant and resentful. Hu (1985) studied the life situations of nonparticipants. They believed that the following factors made it impractical for them to take part in college and university programs: employment responsibilities, inadequate childcare facilities, lack of public transportation, scheduling at busy times, absence of academic counseling, and limited financial resources. Clearly, any programmer who wishes to reach the members of this audience would have to be quite innovative in designing programs to overcome or compensate for these restricting factors. Lamoureux (1977) studied the influence of course length and course cost on enrollment and concluded that prospective participants gave course length more weight than the cost of registration. That outcome may have been influenced by the socioeconomic status of the target audience, and it should thus not be generalized to the members of all social classes. To sum up, every programming decision can be regarded as part of the total marketing design. Programming must consider the life situations of members of the target audience.

Financial Considerations. Those who market a program must know what the financial base is and the extent to which participants will have to bear its costs. For those who are convinced that "you only get what you pay for," a free program is not likely to be appealing. Other people do not take part in activities only because their financial situation leaves nothing for personal educational expenses. To program for each socioeconomic segment of the market, financial planning is essential. The results of that planning must be made known to the potential audience if they are to make informed decisions about participation.

Informing Supportive Publics. As mentioned earlier, the planner is well advised to make the design of the learning activity clear to the prospective audience. In addition to informing the intended audience, the skillful programmer will also take time to interpret the program to third parties who have some influence on participation. If spouses, employers, associates, and other related publics are persuaded that a program has value, they are likely to encourage those in the intended audience to participate. Moreover, their support increases the likelihood that the program will be successful in reaching its goals.

Research on Successful Strategies. Goodnow (1980) studied the demographic characteristics and interests of adult learners in Glen Ellyn, Illinois. She reports that the information obtained was useful in identifying the various market segments and in developing target promotional strategies for each segment. Her experience suggests that, the more complete the knowledge the planner has of the characteristics of the intended audience, the better prepared that planner will be to put together a program that will appeal successfully to the audience.

The American College Testing Program (1983) surveyed 105 college programs aimed at recruiting and retaining adult learners. This survey produced an inventory of experiences, but it did not analyze the most successful methods. Further study of techniques and approaches may be profitable, but the number of factors in each program that needs to be considered is so large as to make comparisons among programs extremely difficult. Clearly, adult education program analysts could do a great deal to increase the level of knowledge about successful practices, but such an accomplishment would require the processing of great quantities of data.

Improving Retention Through Marketing

Retention, like recruitment, can be affected by marketing but not to as great a degree. While the image of the program that is conveyed to the target audience can help to create a demand, the participants who attend class sessions are in a position to compare their direct observations with the claims made by marketers. Complete and accurate information about the program may be effective in discouraging those for whom the course has not been designed from enrolling. At the same time, the factors that have been identified as causes for dropping out have not been directly related to the content or the conduct of the course, especially for participants of low socioeconomic status. Nicholson and Otto (1966) have reported that external or situational reasons are the causes of dropout or noncompletion of program among those of limited means.

What goes on in classrooms or workshop sessions has an influence on dropout, but it is the teacher rather than the program planner who is responsible for maintaining the marketing sensitivity when organizing, conducting, and evaluating the instructional program. The program planner who is alert to the importance of developing a favorable climate for learning may invest some effort in assisting teachers to reach and reflect on the problems of retention and on approaches to the reduction of dropout.

Conclusions and Observations

Marketing, like program planning, calls for the person in charge to secure accurate and detailed information on the intended target audience and to use that information wisely when shaping the message that is to be conveyed to the audience. The program planner or the marketer may be motivated by a desire to serve a particular target group in a variety of ways or to promote a program that is thought to have particularly valuable benefits for participants. If accurate and complete information is conveyed to the intended audience, the audience will have the information that it needs in order to make wise choices regarding the costs and benefits of participation. Having provided the intended audience with complete and honest information, the programmer and the marketer can both anticipate that there will still be some difficulties with retention, particularly for individuals whose social and economic status limits their ability to pursue the programs that they believe to match their needs and interests. Other factors may come into play for those at the other end of the socioeconomic spectrum. Indeed, the role of government in regulating such learning activities as continuing professional education may be expected to exert a marked influence on both recruitment and retention in such programs.

According to Falk (1986, p. 71) "the best marketing tool for a continuing education program is to offer high-quality programs." Although there may be some disagreement about the definition of quality, program development that is sensitive to the felt needs of intended audiences and that openly communicates the full story about the programs being offered will enjoy satisfactory recruitment and retention and play a socially worthwhile role by improving the quality of life for all. Enlightened marketing can enable the adult education program planner to improve both recruitment and retention in programs and ensure that well-planned programs reach and serve the audiences for which they are intended.

References

American College Testing Program. *Attracting and Retaining Adult Learners (ARAL)*. Iowa City, Iowa: American College Testing Program, 1983.

Beder, H. "Basic Concepts and Principles of Marketing." In H. Beder (ed.), *Marketing Continuing Education*. New Directions for Continuing Education, no. 31. San Francisco: Jossey-Bass, 1986.

Buckmaster, A. "Marketing and Market Research for Adult and Continuing Education." Paper presented at the National Adult Education Conference, Milwaukee, Wis., Nov. 1985.

Falk, C. F. "Promoting Continuing Education Programs." In H. Beder (ed.), *Marketing Continuing Education*. New Directions for Continuing Education, no. 31. San Francisco: Jossey-Bass, 1986.

Goodnow, B. "Increasing Enrollment by Better Serving Your Institution's Target Audience Through Benefit Segmentation." Paper presented at the National Adult Education Conference, St. Louis, Mo., Nov. 4, 1980.

Houle, C. O. *The Design of Education*. San Francisco: Jossey-Bass, 1972.

Hu, M. "Determining the Needs and Attitudes of Nontraditional University Students." *College and University*, 1985, 6 (3), 201–209.

Kotler, P. *Marketing for Nonprofit Organizations*. Englewood Cliffs, N.J.: Prentice-Hall, 1975.

Lamoureux, M. E. "Course Length Versus Course Price: Marketing Factors in Program Planning." Paper presented at the 1977 National Adult Education Conference, Detroit, Mich., Oct. 31, 1977.

Mason, R. C. "Locating Continuing Education Programs." In H. Beder (ed.), *Marketing Continuing Education*. New Directions for Continuing Education, no. 31. San Francisco: Jossey-Bass, 1986.

Nicholson, E., and Otto, W. "A Study of Dropouts from Adult Literacy Programs." Paper presented at the 16th National Reading Conference, St. Petersburg, Fla., Dec. 1–3, 1966.

Stern, M. R. "A Disorderly Market." In M. R. Stern (ed.), *Power and Conflict in Continuing Professional Education*. Belmont, Calif.: Wadsworth, 1983.

William S. Griffith is professor of adult education in the Department of Administrative, Adult, and Higher Education at the University of British Columbia, Vancouver, Canada.

This chapter examines how adults decide whether to participate in continuing professional education programs.

Recruiting and Retaining Adult Students in Continuing Professional Education

Brandt W. Pryor

Practitioners of continuing professional education (CPE) are vitally concerned with participation. They often want to increase the rates of participation in their programs or to enhance the quality of participation by making their programs more effective. This chapter describes a model that practitioners can use to accomplish both aims. I begin by sketching some approaches to the understanding of adult participation in education. Next, I describe the model. Last, I show how it can be used to increase the effectiveness of practice in continuing professional education.

Understanding Participation

Much of the research on adult participation in education examines general, rather than professional, continuing education. Although there are important differences between the two areas of practice, these differences are unimportant from the perspective taken by this chapter.

The research on adult participation in education takes one of two basic approaches: the descriptive or the explanatory. Much of the literature on participation consists of descriptive studies, such as the classic work by Johnstone and Rivera (1965). Asking such questions as, Who participates? and How much do they participate? these studies rely heavily on the analysis of differences in the demographic characteristics of participants and nonparticipants. This line of inquiry has produced considerable knowledge about who participates and who does not as well as an understanding of the demographic characteristics, such as level of formal education, that are most closely associated with participation. The knowledge produced by these descriptive studies is a good basis for further research, but as Cross (1981) has pointed out, it falls short of explaining why adults participate in continuing education, and it has limited utility for increasing participation.

Explanatory studies of participation seek to answer the question, Why do adults participate? One school of explanatory researchers has emphasized factors thought to motivate participation. Houle's (1961) seminal study, which found three motivational orientations for participation in continuing education, prompted considerable research on motivators for participation. Boshier (1971, 1977) and other researchers have used factor analysis to determine the underlying structure of the reasons that adults give for their participation in continuing education. Reviewing fourteen such studies, Boshier (1976) concluded that Houle's typology of learning orientations could neither be accepted nor rejected on the basis of those findings. More recently, Boshier and Collins (1985, p. 127) conducted a secondary analysis of data from fifty-four such studies and found only that "Houle's intuition has been partly corroborated."

Other researchers have examined the reasons that adults give for not participating in continuing education. Scanlan and Darkenwald (1984) and Darkenwald and Valentine (1985) used factor analysis to explore the underlying structure of perceived barriers to participation. Both studies found conceptually meaningful deterrent factors. Their authors argued persuasively that deterrent factors as well as motivating factors should be included in theories of participation in continuing education.

A number of scholars, including Rubenson (1976), Cross (1981), and Cookson (1986), have included both motivators and barriers in their exploratory models. Each model is proposed as a way of integrating current knowledge in order to increase our understanding of participation and as a basis for research and the development of theory. Each model includes both the psychological and the sociological variables that descriptive research has shown to be relevant to participation in continuing education. The psychological variables are defined as the variables relatively close in time to the phenomenon of participation—such factors as attitudes, beliefs, and perceptions of social pressure to participate. The sociological variables are defined as the variables relatively removed in the time from participation—such factors as level of formal education, income, ethnicity, and employment. Each model describes the ways in which the variables influence one another and affect participation. Despite some differences in their variables and interrelationships, the models generally show the psychological variables as mediating the sociological variables. That is, sociological variables have their effects on participation only by first affecting the psychological variables. For example, the sociological variable of previous formal education influences participation by first affecting attitudes toward education and beliefs about educational efficacy.

In the long term, these models may be most useful by providing a comprehensive understanding of participation in continuing education. In the short term, their very inclusiveness may be a limitation. The large number of variables and the complex and sometimes unclear relationships among them are likely to inhibit research that relies on them. At the current stage of our knowledge, it may be useful to focus research on the more proximal psychological variables that influence participation in continuing education. This emphasis appears to have some benefits for researchers, but its clearest payoff is for practitioners of continuing professional education, in that the psychological variables are the only ones that practitioners can have any hope of influencing. Attitudes, beliefs, and perceptions of social pressure to participate in continuing professional education can be influenced so as to increase participation. The knowledge of why professionals do or do not choose to participate can provide information that program developers can use to enhance the quality of participation.

A Model for Understanding Participation

Fishbein (1967) and Fishbein and Ajzen (1975) have developed a model that explains how people decide to perform or not to perform specific behaviors. Over the last two decades, the model has been used successfully to predict and explain behavioral intentions and behavior in a variety of areas. For example, it has been used to explain intentions to participate in eight leisure time activities (Ajzen and Fishbein, 1969), to use birth control pills (Jaccard and Davidson, 1972), and to vote in an election (Fishbein and Coombs, 1974). The diversity of the successful applications suggest that the model may be useful in explaining why professionals choose to participate in continuing professional education.

According to the model, the performance of a given behavior, such as registering for a CPE program, is caused by an intention to perform that behavior. An intention to register for a CPE program is caused by a positive attitude toward registering or by a perception of social pressure to register. (*Attitude* is defined as a feeling of liking or disliking for something: an object, a person, or a behavior.) The model is concerned with an attitude toward a behavior, that is, with how people feel about performing the behavior. The social pressure variable is called a *subjective norm* both to distinguish it from general social norms and because it constitutes subjective perceptions—what people think their important others want them to do with regard to a specific behavior.

All other factors that might influence intention, such as age and level of education, are mediated by attitude and subjective norm. This means that these other factors can affect behavioral intention only by first influencing either attitude or subjective norm or by their relative importance in forming intention. Attitude is often more important than subjective norm, but the importance varies with specific behaviors and populations.

For example, the intentions of oral surgeons to register for a continuing professional education program were found to be determined virtually by attitude; subjective norm made no significant contribution to intention (Pryor, 1987). It seems likely that the same would be true for other professionals in private practice. However, subjective norm may be more important for the formation of the behavioral intentions of professionals employed within hierarchical organizations, especially those who report to direct superiors. Support for this hypothesis was provided by a recent study of library staff members that found intentions to participate in a CPE program to be influenced significantly by subjective norm (Pryor, 1988).

Physicians and nurses directly employed by care units, teachers, and police officers are three categories of professionals who might be influenced by perceptions of normative pressure. For example, the intentions of police officers to register for CPE might be influenced by their perceptions of what their superiors wanted them to do. The perceived expectations of partners, other coworkers, and families might also be important in the formation of their intentions to register for CPE.

Therefore, it is necessary to determine the relative importance of attitude and subjective norm for the specific behavior and population of interest before planning a strategy aimed at changing intentions. Estimates of the relative importance of each variable are obtained through multiple regression of the intention measure on measures of attitude and subjective norm. Figure 1 illustrates the relationships among behavior, intention, attitude, and subjective norm.

Attitude toward the behavior is formed by a set of beliefs about the outcomes that can be expected from performing the behavior and by an evaluation of each outcome. For example, as physicians review a national CPE program announcement, they begin to form beliefs about the outcomes of registering. These beliefs can include such things as "It would cost a lot of money," "I would learn a lot," and "I would see old friends at the program." Different physicians will hold these beliefs with different degrees of certainty, and some will not hold them at all.

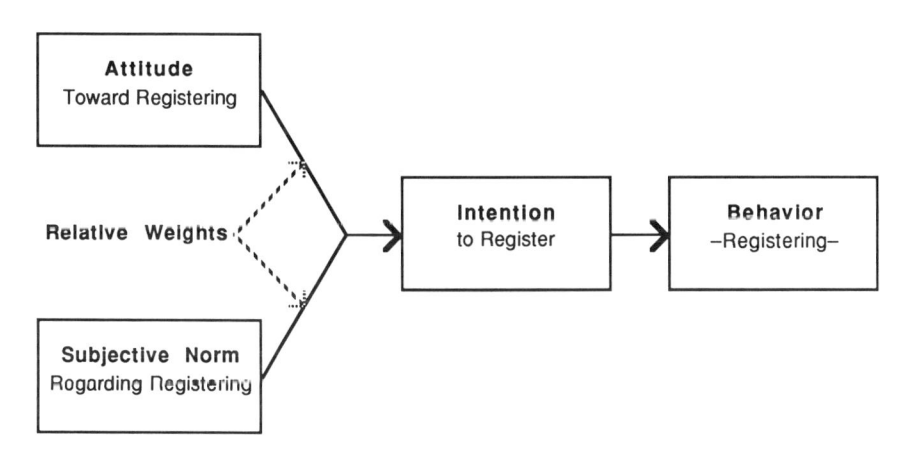

Figure 1. Relationships Among Behavior, Intention, Attitude, and Subjective Norm

```
┌─────────────────┐
│    Attitude     │
│ Toward Registering │
└─────────────────┘
                  ╲
                   ╲
Relative Weights    ╲    ┌─────────────┐      ┌─────────────┐
                     ──▶ │  Intention  │ ───▶ │  Behavior   │
                    ╱    │ to Register │      │ –Registering– │
                   ╱     └─────────────┘      └─────────────┘
                  ╱
┌─────────────────┐
│ Subjective Norm │
│Regarding Registering│
└─────────────────┘
```

In addition to the beliefs about outcomes, each outcome is evaluated. Some physicians may evaluate a chance to see old friends as extremely good because they want to collaborate on a research project or compare notes on a difficult case. Some may view spending a lot of money as slightly bad, while others may see it as extremely bad. Still others may view a high registration fee as quite good, seeing it as an indication of a high-quality program. Figure 2 depicts the relation between outcome beliefs, outcome evaluations, and attitude formation.

Subjective norm is formed by beliefs that certain important others think the person should or should not perform the behavior and by the person's motivation to comply with these important others. These others are individuals or groups that are important to the person. As the physicians in our example read the program brochure, they will also form subjective impressions of whether those who are important to them think they should register. Some physicians might form the belief that their families think they should not register for the national CPE program, because that would cause them to be away from home. Physicians in group practice might form the belief that their partners would want them to register because the program teaches a new surgical procedure in which they are interested. Physicians directly employed by hospitals might think their superiors would not want them to register because the superiors have been trying to reduce costs.

While the physicians form their beliefs about the wishes of referents as they read the brochure, the motivation to comply with the referents preexists the reading of the brochure. Some physicians may want very much to do what their superiors think they should do and not care much

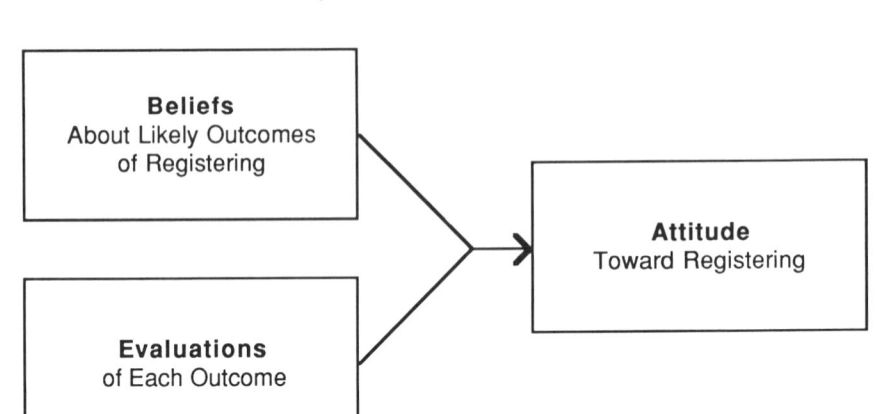

Figure 2. The Effect of Outcome Beliefs and Evaluations on Attitude Formation

```
┌─────────────────────┐
│      Beliefs        │
│  About Likely       │╲
│  Outcomes of        │ ╲
│  Registering        │  ╲
└─────────────────────┘   ╲      ┌─────────────────────┐
                           ╲     │     Attitude        │
                            ──→  │  Toward Registering │
                           ╱     │                     │
┌─────────────────────┐   ╱      └─────────────────────┘
│    Evaluations      │  ╱
│   of Each Outcome   │ ╱
│                     │╱
└─────────────────────┘
```

about their families' opinions. Other physicians may be concerned about what their partners in private practice think about their registering and be relatively indifferent to the view of the American Medical Association. The combination of the strength of beliefs about the referents' desires with the motivation to comply with each referent produces a general sense of social pressure to register or not to register for the program. Figure 3 depicts the relation between normative beliefs, motivation to comply, and subjective norm.

Over the past two decades, the model has been used successfully to predict and explain behavioral intentions. Numerous studies have shown that behavioral intentions are excellent predictors of actual behavior (Fishbein, 1972). McArdle (1972) demonstrated that the understanding of behavioral intentions provided by the model makes it possible to change both intention and behavior in the desired direction. Lutz (1973) showed that attitude could be changed by changing the beliefs that form attitude.

Grotelueschen and Caulley (1977) suggested that the model could be applied in research on participation in continuing professional education. Four years later, Ray (1981) reported the results of a study that applied certain variables of the model in an attempt to understand the formation of intentions to participate in CPE. The variables of the model used in that study explained only 10 percent of the variance in the intention measure—no more than demographic variables had already explained (Anderson and Darkenwald, 1979). Although Ray (1981) called for further research on the model, his findings may have caused other researchers to doubt the model's ability to predict and explain participation in CPE.

Figure 3. The Effect of Normative Beliefs and Motivation to Comply on Formation of Subjective Norm

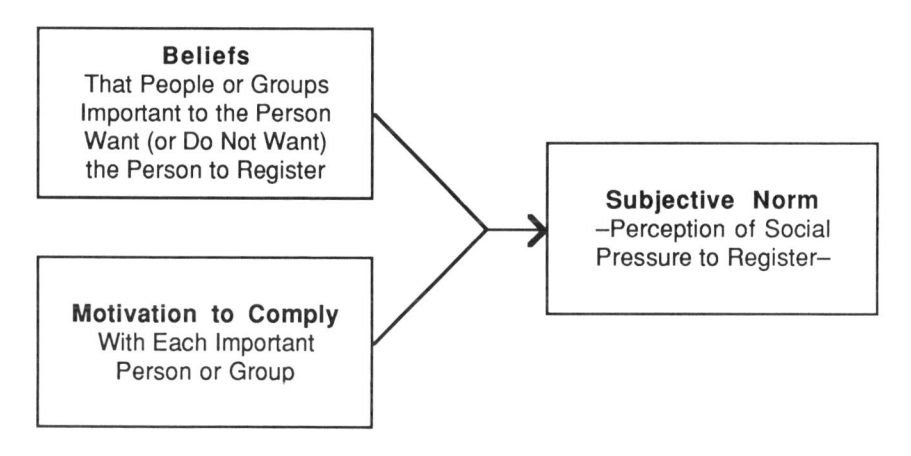

```
┌─────────────────────────┐
│        Beliefs          │
│ That People or Groups   │
│ Important to the Person │──┐
│ Want (or Do Not Want)   │  │    ┌──────────────────────┐
│ the Person to Register  │  │    │  Subjective Norm     │
└─────────────────────────┘  └──▶ │ –Perception of Social│
                                  │   Pressure to Register–│
┌─────────────────────────┐  ┌──▶ └──────────────────────┘
│  Motivation to Comply   │  │
│   With Each Important   │──┘
│     Person or Group     │
└─────────────────────────┘
```

However, one study is an insufficient test of a model. My first study (Pryor, 1987), which applied the entire model, found it to explain more than 41 percent of the variance in intentions to register for a CPE program. Three subsequent studies of intentions to participate in CPE (Pryor, 1988), which applied direct measures of attitude and subjective norm, accounted for considerably higher amounts of the variance in intentions. It appears likely that further research using the entire model will confirm these preliminary findings that the model is successful in predicting and explaining intentions to register for CPE programs.

A Model for Increasing and Enhancing Participation

This section shows how practitioners can use the model just described to increase rates of participation in their programs and to enhance the quality of participation by professionals.

Increasing Participation. Once professionals become aware of the existence of a relevant CPE program, they begin to form positive or negative intentions about registering for the program. Generally, as the information that they have about the program increases, the number of outcome and normative beliefs that they have, the strength of these beliefs, and the strength of their intentions all increase.

To increase participation, the practitioner must provide professionals with information that influences their intentions in a positive direction. Efforts aimed at changing intention can be directed to the outcome beliefs that affect attitude negatively or toward the normative beliefs that affect subjective norm negatively. If attitude and norm have equal importance in forming intention, change efforts can target both outcome and normative beliefs. Let us look first at how negative attitudes toward registering for a CPE program are formed and then at how the model might be used to change them in a positive direction.

Formation and Change of Attitude. Negative attitudes toward registering for a CPE program involve a feeling of dislike for registering for the program, a perception that it would not be a good idea to do so. Negative attitudes are formed when negative beliefs about the outcomes of registering outweigh the positive beliefs about outcomes.

For the purposes of illustration, let us consider a hypothetical group of nurses. The nurses in our group have just received a rather sketchy preliminary flier announcing a national CPE program. How do the nurses decide whether to register for the program?

As the nurses read the flier, they begin to form beliefs about the likely outcomes of registering for the program. They believe that some of these outcomes are more likely than others to result from registering, and they evaluate the outcomes somewhat differently. We can measure the strength with which each belief is held—that is, the certainty that the outcome would result from registering. For example, we can measure the strength of the belief "Registering for the program will lead to improving my care of patients" on a seven-point probability scale:

Likely (+3) : (+2) : (+1) : (0) : (-1) : (-2) : (-3) Unlikely
      extremely quite slightly neither slightly quite extremely

We can also measure the nurses' evaluations of the outcomes of registering. For example, we can measure their evaluation of the outcome "Improving my care of patients" on a seven-point evaluative scale:

Good (+3) : (+2) : (+1) : (0) : (-1) : (-2) : (-3) Bad
     extremely quite slightly neither slightly quite extremely

Table 1 represents the outcome beliefs of our hypothetical nurses. Their beliefs are somewhat negative, as the -6 total of their belief strength-evaluation products shows. What information could a practitioner include in the final program brochure to change the nurses' attitudes in a positive direction? Since attitudes are formed by the set of outcome beliefs and evaluations, efforts to change attitudes must focus on changing outcome beliefs, evaluations, or both. Let us look first at ways of changing the beliefs about outcomes.

The outcome beliefs that determine a negative attitude toward registering can be accurate or inaccurate. If the negatively evaluated outcome beliefs are accurate, the program might need to be changed. By eliminating or reducing the aspects of the program that lead to negatively evalu-

Table 1. Beliefs of Hypothetical Nurses About the Outcomes of Registering for a Continuing Professional Education Program

Outcome	Belief Strength	Evaluation	Product
Improving patient care	+1	+3	+3
Gaining useful information	+2	+3	+6
Hearing knowledgeable speakers	+2	+2	+4
Listening to lectures all day	+2	-2	-4
Leaving my family	+3	-3	-9
Hearing material over my head	+2	-3	-6
Total			-6

ated outcome beliefs, the practitioner can change attitudes in a positive direction.

If the negatively evaluated beliefs about outcomes are inaccurate, practitioners must correct the false impressions.

There are two ways of changing the beliefs about outcomes that predispose the target audience to a negative attitude. The first is to reduce the strength with which one or more of the beliefs is held; that is, to reduce the certainty that people have that the behavior will have a given outcome. The second is by adding new beliefs about outcomes that the target audience is likely to evaluate both strongly and positively.

With respect to the first way, the product scores in Table 1 highlight the beliefs and evaluations that make the largest negative contributions to the attitudes of our hypothetical nurses toward registering.

Two beliefs make the largest negative contributions: the belief that registering would lead to "leaving my family" and the belief that registering would lead to "hearing material that is over my head." The first belief is accurate, in that participation in a national program requires considerable travel for most registrants. Regional programs that reduce travel time for participants might be considered.

The second belief—that registering would result in "hearing material over my head"—may or may not be accurate. If the belief is accurate, the practitioner can conclude that the program is too advanced for most members of the target audience and that improvements both in market segmentation and in needs assessment are in order. The practitioner may wish to revise the level of instruction so that it more closely fits the needs of the nurses and to emphasize this in the final program brochure.

If the belief about the difficulty level of the program is inaccurate, program promotion and advertising can correct the false impression in the final brochure by specifying the prerequisites in education and experience that participants need. The brochure might also stress the speakers' abilities to communicate clearly and effectively with nurses. By reducing the strength of the nurses' belief that they would hear material that was over their head from *quite likely* (+2) to *slightly likely* (+1), the practitioner could reduce the negative contribution of that outcome belief to attitude by half.

The third belief that makes a negative contribution to attitude is the belief that registering for the program will lead to "listening to lectures all day." If the belief is accurate, program planners may wish to replace or alternate lecture sessions with other forms of learning activities. If they do, the final brochure should stress the fact. However, the belief may be inaccurate. Our hypothetical nurses may rarely have experienced CPE programs that offered instruction in other forms and thus automatically associate CPE with lectures. In this case, the final brochure must emphasize the nonlecture instructional delivery methods used in the program.

The second way of altering the belief-evaluation set in a positive direction is to add new beliefs that the target audience will evaluate strongly and positively. For example, nurses are showing increasing interest in working in nontraditional settings, such as private practice, management of health care delivery, and ownership of health care businesses (Bezold and Carlson, 1986). It might be possible to alter the outcome belief set of our hypothetical nurses in a positive direction by adding a component on "Going Independent" to the program. The final program brochure could emphasize that this component provided information about establishing a private practice or business in health care and about gaining entry to managerial positions.

If our nurses believed that it was *extremely likely* (+3) that they would learn about "Going Independent" as a result of registering for the program and if they evaluated learning about going independent as *extremely good* (+3), the addition of this new belief, which makes a strong positive contribution (+9) to their attitudes, would more than offset the existing belief-evaluation products total (-6). Indeed, the new total (+3) would be considerably more positive.

Formation and Change of Subjective Norm. There may be instances in which normative pressure is more important than attitude in forming professionals' intentions to perform a given behavior, such as registering for a CPE program. For example, the intentions of our hypothetical nurses not to register for the program might be based primarily on negative subjective norm, that is, on a perception that those persons or groups most important to them wanted them not to register for the program. Table 2 depicts the subjective norm for our hypothetical nurses. We can measure the strength with which each of the normative beliefs is held. For example, we can measure the strength of the normative belief "My

Table 2. Normative Beliefs of Hypothetical Nurses About Registering for a Continuing Professional Education Program

Referent	Belief Strength	Motivation to Comply	Product
My direct supervisor	+1	+7	+7
My peers at work	+1	+1	+1
My professional society	+2	+5	+10
My children	-2	+3	-6
My spouse	-3	+7	-21
Total			-9

direct supervisor wants me to register for the program" on a seven-point probability scale:

Likely (+3) : (+2) : (+1) : (0) : (-1) : (-2) : (-3) Unlikely
       extremely quite slightly neither slightly quite extremely

We can also measure the nurses' motivations to comply with the perceived wishes of each referent. For example, we can measure their motivation to comply with their direct supervisor on a seven-point probability scale:

Likely (+7) : (+6) : (+5) : (+4) : (+3) : (+2) : (+1) Unlikely
       extremely quite slightly neither slightly quite extremely

Notice that the scores in the Motivation to Comply column are all positive. Although it is unlikely that the nurses will not be motivated to comply with some referents, such as their children, it is unlikely that they will be motivated to do the opposite of what any referent wants.

Table 2 highlights the referents that make the largest negative contribution to subjective norm. In our example, spouse and children are the only negative referents. However, their contributions are quite different, since the nurses are much more motivated to comply with spouses than they are with children.

There are three ways of changing the subjective norm in a positive direction. The first focuses on negative referents with whom members of the target audience are strongly motivated to comply, such as the spouses of our nurses. This approach involves decreasing the strength of normative beliefs. For example, information in the final brochure could emphasize the benefits to spouses of the nurses' registering. Opportunities for advancement or increased pay might be appropriate benefits.

The second way of changing the subjective norm focuses on positive referents with whom the members of the target audience are strongly motivated to comply—for our nurses the direct supervisor. This approach involves increasing the strength of normative beliefs. Although the nurses in our example believe that their direct supervisors want them to register and they are highly motivated to comply with their direct supervisors, this belief is so weak (*slightly likely*) that it makes a very small positive contribution to subjective norm. In this instance, the final brochure could emphasize the benefits to supervisors from having the nurses register for the program. For example, participation in the program might make the nurses more efficient, or it might make them able to perform with less supervision.

The third way of changing the subjective norm focuses on making the target audience aware of new referents with whom they are motivated to comply and whom they perceive as wanting them to perform the behavior. For our hypothetical nurses, such new referents might be their patients or perhaps former teachers and mentors from nursing school.

Enhancing Participation. There appear to be at least three ways in which the model described in this chapter can be used to enhance the quality of participation by improving programs. Use of the model can enhance current practices in needs assessment, in formative evaluation, and in summative evaluation.

Regarding needs assessment, Darkenwald (1977) has emphasized the importance for program design and promotion of understanding the motivation of adults to participate in educational programs. At a minimum, the needs assessment process in CPE determines learning needs perceived by members of the target professional audience. The perceptions of clients, experts, and others can also be sought. The model suggests that needs assessment should determine not only the learning needs perceived by each group but the relative importance that each group assigns to each need. Such information would be invaluable for making decisions about what to include in a program and about the proportion of time to be devoted to each learning need.

Formative evaluation focuses on program improvements. It often measures the satisfaction of participants with intuitively selected aspects of the program. Such evaluations could be improved by use of the model's attitudinal component, including beliefs about the outcomes of participating in the program and evaluations of each outcome. Use of the attitudinal component would help practitioners to understand which program component made the largest contributions to negative attitudes and which components made the largest contributions to positive attitudes about having participated in the program.

Summative evaluation focuses on the value of a program. It can be used to make decisions about program continuation. A question of increasing concern for CPE is whether programs make a difference in the professional practices of participants (Holt and Courtney, 1985). It is likely that demands for accountability, especially in professions with mandatory CPE, will cause the number of impact evaluations to increase. Certain evaluation approaches might well be able to assess program impact in a valid way yet provide little or no information useful for program redesign.

Use of the model described here could enable evaluation studies to address the issue of impact in a formative as well as a summative manner. For example, the evaluation could examine the intentions of recent participants to use the knowledge gained in the program. Professionals with positive intentions to use the knowledge could be compared with professionals with negative intentions to use the knowledge. An understanding of the beliefs that made the largest positive and negative contributions to intention could be valuable for program redesign aimed at enhancing the use of new knowledge gained through participation in CPE.

The model discussed in this chapter appears to have considerable potential for strengthening practice in continuing professional education. It has been successfully applied in an effort to understand the formation of intentions to register for a CPE program, and it has potential for increasing rates of participation and advancing needs assessment and evaluation. Its standardized measures of variables give us an opportunity to build an integrated and cumulative body of knowledge about participation in CPE. This body of knowledge would increase our understanding of how the model could be used most effectively to increase and enhance participation in CPE.

References

Ajzen, I., and Fishbein, M. "The Prediction of Behavioral Intentions in a Choice Situation." *Journal of Experimental Social Psychology*, 1969, *5*, 400-416.

Anderson, R. E., and Darkenwald, G. G. *Participation and Persistence in American Adult Education*. New York: College Board, 1979.

Bezold, C., and Carlson, R. "Nursing in the Twenty-First Century: Conclusion." *Journal of Professional Nursing*, 1986, *3* (1), 69-71.

Boshier, R. W. "Motivational Orientations of Adult Education Participants: A Factor-Analytic Exploration of Houle's Typology." *Adult Education*, 1971, *21*, 3-26.

Boshier, R. W. "Factor Analysts at Large: A Critical Review of the Motivational Orientation Literature." *Adult Education*, 1976, *26*, 22-47.

Boshier, R. W. "Motivational Orientations Revisited: Life-Space Motives and the Education Participation Scale." *Adult Education*, 1977, *27*, 89-115.

Boshier, R. W., and Collins, J. B. "The Houle Typology After Twenty-Two Years: A Large-Scale Empirical Test." *Adult Education Quarterly*, 1985, *35*, 113-130.

Cookson, P. S. "A Framework for Theory and Research on Adult Education Participation." *Adult Education Quarterly*, 1986, *36* (3), 130-141.

Cross, K. P. *Adults as Learners: Increasing Participation and Facilitating Learning*. San Francisco: Jossey-Bass, 1981.

Darkenwald, G. G. "Why Adults Participate in Education: Some Implications for Program Development of Research on Motivational Orientations." Speech presented to the faculty of the University Extension Division, Rutgers University, Jan. 26, 1977. (ED 135 992)

Darkenwald, G. G., and Valentine, T. "Factor Structure of Deterrents to Public Participation in Adult Education." *Adult Education Quarterly*, 1985, *35*, 177-193.

Fishbein, M. "Attitude and the Prediction of Behavior." In M. Fishbein (ed.), *Readings in Attitude Theory and Measurement.* New York: Wiley, 1967.

Fishbein, M. "The Search for Attitude-Behavioral Consistency." In J. B. Cohen (ed.), *Behavioral Science Foundations of Consumer Behavior.* New York: Free Press, 1972.

Fishbein, M., and Ajzen, I. *Belief, Attitude, Intention, and Behavior: An Introduction to Theory and Research.* Reading, Mass.: Addison-Wesley, 1975.

Fishbein, M., and Coombs, F. S. "Basis for Decision: An Attitudinal Analysis of Voting Behavior." *Journal of Applied Social Psychology*, 1974, *4*, 95-124.

Grotelueschen, A. D., and Caulley, D. N. "A Model for Studying Determinants of Intention to Participate in Continuing Professional Education." *Adult Education*, 1977, *28*, 22-37.

Holt, M. E., and Courtney, B. C. "An Examination of Impact Evaluations." *Continuum*, 1985, *49*, 23-35.

Houle, C. O. *The Inquiring Mind.* Madison: University of Wisconsin Press, 1961.

Jaccard, J., and Davidson, A. R. "A Comparison of Two Models of Social Behavior: Results of a Survey Sample." *Sociometry*, 1972, *38*, 497-517.

Johnstone, J. W., and Rivera, R. J. *Volunteers for Learning.* Chicago: Aldine, 1965.

Lutz, R. J. "Cognitive Change and Attitude Change: A Validation Study." Unpublished doctoral dissertation, University of Illinois, Urbana, 1973.

McArdle, J. B. "Positive and Negative Communications and Subsequent Attitude and Behavior Change in Alcoholics." Unpublished doctoral dissertation, University of Illinois, Urbana-Champaign, 1972.

Pryor, B. W. "Psychological Determinants of Oral Surgeons' Intentions to Participate in Continuing Professional Education." Unpublished doctoral dissertation, University of Illinois, Urbana-Champaign, 1987.

Pryor, B. W. *Final Report to the Illinois State Library: Career Development Workshops for Library Staff—A Multimedia Approach.* Champaign, Ill.: Lincoln Trial Library System, 1988.

Ray, R. O. "Examining Motivation to Participate in Continuing Education: An Investigation of Recreation Professionals." *Journal of Leisure Research*, 1981, *1*, 66-75.

Rubenson, K. "Recruitment in Adult Education: A Research Strategy." Unpublished report, Department of Education and Psychology, Linkoping University, 1976.

Scanlan, C. S., and Darkenwald, G. G. "Identifying Deterrents to Participation in Continuing Education." *Adult Education Quarterly*, 1984, *34*, 155-166.

Brandt W. Pryor, an educational consultant in St. Louis, Missouri, has been a member of the research faculty of the University of Illinois at Urbana-Champaign. His special interests are program development and evaluation and participation in continuing education.

It appears that adult undergraduates are here to stay, and institutions of higher education have become more responsive to their needs. This chapter reports on some successful approaches to recruiting, admitting, and retaining the members of this population.

Recruiting and Retaining Adult Students in Higher Education

Jovita Martin Ross

One does not need to be a continuing educator to be aware that adults are attending college in record numbers. The popular press and other media offer frequent reminders of this phenomenon. Movies have spoofed the trials and tribulations of the older-than-average college student. However, for the adult learner taking college classes and for institutions hoping to offset declining enrollments among students of traditional age, adult college attendance is a more serious matter. Significant resources are committed to recruiting adult students. This chapter will examine not only how these students are recruited and why they come but also the range of institutional accommodations that facilitate the admission and retention of these students. While institutional responses to adult students extend from business as usual to the development of nontraditional forms of higher education, such as external degree programs, this chapter focuses on programs within traditional institutions of higher education attended by full-time or part-time students.

P. S. Cookson (ed.). *Recruiting and Retaining Adult Students.*
New Directions for Continuing Education, no. 41. San Francisco: Jossey-Bass, Spring 1989.

Trends in Participation

At the beginning of this decade, Magarell (1981) noted that at least one-third of all college students were twenty-five years of age or older. Although the characteristics distinguishing traditional-age students from students older than average have become increasingly blurred as increasing numbers of young students stop out, work while in college, and attend part-time, most recent discussions of the adult student in higher education use age twenty-five as a convention. Enrollment by students twenty-five and older increased 26 percent between 1975 and 1979, while enrollment among younger students increased by only 10 percent (Magarell, 1981). With the population of thirty- to forty-four-year-olds expected to increase by 42 percent during the 1980s (Hodgkinson, 1983), many institutions have been pleased to hear that an adult market is expected to offset enrollment declines due to smaller birth cohorts among traditional-age college students. The greatest increases in participation have been among women, with enrollments by women over thirty-five climbing 66.8 percent in five years and enrollments among women between twenty-five and thirty-four up 58.7 percent. At the same time, enrollments by men between twenty-five and thirty-four have declined slightly (Magarell, 1981).

A number of factors have influenced this trend in adult enrollments. These factors include changing social norms regarding women's education and participation in the labor force, changing economic conditions and rising standards of living, increasing acceptance of the notion of lifelong learning, and increasing requirements for occupation-related learning during adulthood. Many men and women now feel it necessary to obtain a college degree in order to meet the requirements for new careers, advance within an existing career, or simply maintain a current position. There is increasing acceptance—even an emerging expectation—that women spend part of their adult years involved in work outside the home as well as in the home. To get the kinds of jobs they desire, a degree is desirable. Many adults also aspire to the sense of accomplishment associated with higher education, often by continuing studies interrupted years before.

Indeed, adults' motives for participation in higher education are often quite varied. Apps (1981) identifies six categories of motivation. Occupation-related motives—career entry, career change, job promotion, and mandatory continuing education—came first. College faculty whom he interviewed perceived these to be the most common motives in the adult students whom they taught. Sewall (1984) found that 65 percent of the 1,343 adult degree students whom he surveyed identified career motivations as very important. Next, Apps (1981) indicates, adults choose college because it is socially acceptable; the women's movement and growing acceptance of lifelong learning have lowered the barriers that prevented many adults from attending college. Life enhancement is the third category of motives that Apps (1981) identifies. In Sewall's (1984) sample, 61 percent cited a desire to learn as very important, while 51 percent wanted the satisfaction of earning a degree. A change in life situation is Apps's (1981) fourth category. Aslanian and Brickell (1980) first popularized the notion of triggers for adult learning, and numerous other authors have explored the role of both positive and negative life changes as triggers motivating the return to higher education (Ross, 1988; Sewall, 1984). Apps (1981) describes the societal premium placed on the college degree as the fifth category. A degree seems necessary for many jobs now, and certificates or advanced degrees are often part of continuing education for career advancement. Last, Apps (1981) notes, active recruitment of adult students by higher eduation institutions is itself a source of motivation.

There is considerable speculation as to whether these trends can be expected to continue through the 1990s. Bishop and Van Dyk (1977) echo predictions that the adult market will be drained as the reservoir of females desiring a college education dries up and as Vietnam veterans deplete their educational benefits. However, O'Connor and Aasheim (1985) point out that only 14 percent of Americans have college degrees, which suggests that a large market remains to be tapped. Hodgkinson (1983) notes that institutions of higher education serve only 12 million adults, while another 46 million continue their postsecondary learning in such sectors as the military or business and industry. He maintains that college enrollments will remain stable despite the 25 percent drop in population in the eighteen- to twenty-four-year-old age group if only 25 percent of the adults now being served elsewhere decide to participate in higher education.

Recruiting Adult Students

Many institutions of higher learning have stepped up their efforts to recruit members of this potential market. Between 1979 and 1985, the proportion of institutions actively recruiting adults increased within each of the four major institutional categories: In two-year public institutions, it was up 29 percent, from 54 percent to 83 percent. In two-year private institutions, it was up 24 percent, from 40 percent to 64 percent. In four-year public institutions, the figure increased by 31 percent, from 56 per cent to 87 percent, and in four-year private institutions by 31 percent, from 48 percent to 79 percent ("More Institutional Recruitment," 1987).

Some have criticized such aggressive recruitment of adult learners. Of the critics, O'Connor and Aasheim (1985, p. 9) observe that "Traditional educators seem to believe that recruitment of adults into traditional educational programs will result ultimately in the spread to lock step schooling and the development of an overcredentialized society." They also report concerns about academic hucksterism among institutions that compromise academic standards by virtually selling credentials through liberalized credit-granting policies. Yet, while numerous diploma mills can be identified, most institutions offering alternative means of acquiring credits do so in an honest attempt to serve adult learners. O'Connor and Aasheim's (1985) final concern is the growing suspicion that colleges are more interested in meeting their own needs for survival than they are in the needs of the adult students whom they recruit.

This concern can be addressed if institutions heed the advice of Gallien (1986) that those who want to market a continuing education program must begin with a program worth marketing and develop a marketing program that recognizes adults' wants and needs. In addition to program content that is relevant to adult needs, scheduling must take the family and work obligations common to most adult students into account (Thompson, 1985). Supplementary services that address the needs of adults are another important recruitment tool, as indicated by the success of the Women's Project at C. W. Post's Brentwood campus (Murphy and Achtziger, 1982). The services that appealed to potential women students there included a pre-entry workshop series, a childcare discount arranged with a local childcare center, a support group, and a special scholarship program. Mark and DeWees (1984) indicate that the Experiential Learning Program at Ohio University has served as a recruitment tool by granting credit for prior learning to potential adult students who enroll in a course called "Portfolio Development."

In addition to appropriate programs and convenient scheduling, successful recruitment of adult students can be facilitated by research regarding potential target audiences. Both external mapping and internal mapping were used to develop a marketing plan for the Pitt Community College (1985) in Greenville, North Carolina. External mapping identified five target groups: senior citizens, educational and workforce re-entry men and women, displaced homemakers, the occupational mobile, and the technical scholar. The last group consisted of individuals from business and industry who might attend classes to further a skill. An advisory board assisted the community college administration in identifying the most effective recruitment strategies for each of these subgroups as well as in establishing the best ways of reaching white males, white females, black males, and black females within the community. Surveys soliciting student perceptions regarding activities, programs, costs, faculty-student interaction, counseling services, daycare, and other areas of concern comprised the internal mapping strategy. Hirsh (1986) includes both in-class surveys and focus group interviews among the research strategies used as part of developing a recruitment plan at Muhlenberg College.

Gallien (1986) indicates that currently enrolled students can be among the best spokespersons for conveying the message that a program effectively meets the needs of its adult students. In fact, word of mouth is probably one of the best recruitment techniques (Gallien, 1986; Campbell and Spiro, 1982). A survey conducted at the State University of New York College at Brockport indicated that most continuing education students had learned of the program through personal contact, either with students or faculty and staff. Relatively few recalled receiving direct mail program announcements. Fewer than 25 percent of the students recalled any media advertisement. For both students and the members of a community sample, the newspaper was the most effective of the media sources. Gallien (1986) also emphasizes the value of personalized contact over media promotion campaigns. She suggests information sessions, direct mail, and contacts through the workplace and community colleges as ways of personalizing the contact with potential students.

In summary, the key to effective recruitment of adult students begins with a program that is tailored to their needs. Research detailing those needs can be carried out both through external mapping of segments of the local community and through studies of currently enrolled students. Once the target groups have been identified, personalized contacts seem to yield the highest returns.

Admitting Adult Students

A variety of considerations face the institution that hopes to admit adult students while upholding traditional academic standards. Some adults lack the traditional high school diploma. Credits offered for transfer may have been obtained years before. Finally, the traditional measures used to predict academic success may not be the best predictors of adult performance. High school GPA may not reflect the current ability and motivation of adult students (Cotten and Stock, 1985). Test-taking anxiety can affect performance on the standardized tests taken for college entrance. Recommendations from teachers may be unobtainable or meaningless after years individuals have spent away from academic study. Apart from admissions criteria, certain admissions procedures and practices may be inappropriate for the adult student. Consider the adult's response to an admissions form that asks for parental consent or the impression made by an institutional bulletin that makes no mention of special services for adult students. The admissions decisions made by institutions and the institutional choices made by adult students are affected by a myriad of factors related to the admissions process.

An examination of selected institutional practices reveals methods of responding to these challenges. The problem of the missing high school diploma does not appear to pose a problem for most institutions. Hexter and Andersen (1986) report that 92 percent of the institutions surveyed in a nationally representative sample admit students without a high school diploma. Most accept a high school equivalency certificate based on the General Educational Development (GED) test; about 40 percent accept an adult high school diploma. Ninety-seven percent of the responding institutions permit credit for course work, examinations, or other learning acquired outside formal postsecondary education. The most commonly accepted way of granting credit for extrainstitutional learning is by exam (93 percent); 87 percent of the responding institutions accept the College Board's College-Level Examination Program (CLEP). Seventy-seven percent grant credit for courses taken in the military, while 38 percent give credit for courses taken in business and industry. Slightly more than one-third of the institutions use other assessment procedures—portfolio assessment, faculty committees, occupational licences or certificates—to grant credit for prior learning. However, for almost all forms of alternative credit, credit was granted far less often than the liberal policies themselves would suggest. We could ask whether ignorance of these options among adult students is the primary cause, or whether institutional red tape and failure to publicize options plays the more important role.

With regard to unavailable and outdated high school transcripts, some institutions admit adult students on a provisional basis. In essence, these students are given a chance to prove that they are capable of success. A survey of thirteen four-year campuses in the University of Wisconsin system (Wisconsin Assessment Center, 1983) revealed that, while most adults were admitted under regular admission requirements, a variety of practices made some form of provisional or special admission possible for almost all adults who did not meet those criteria.

A study to identify accurate preadmission predictors of adult student success was conducted at Saint Catherine College (Thieman and Marsh-Williams, 1984). Biographical data, academic records, a test of written English, ratings of self-concept and support from family and others, and a self-report of the use of leisure time served as measures. The best single predictor of GPA was performance on the Test of Standard Written English. Marital status was also predictive for this all-female sample, with married women having higher GPAs. The authors postulate that support from spouses, both of an emotional and an instrumental nature, may be crucial. Four prior academic factors were also significantly correlated with GPA: high school rank, verbal and math college entrance test scores, and prior college GPA. Scores on the Academic Self-Concept Scale (ASCS-R) also were correlated with GPA. Noting the value of the writing test and the self-concept scale, the authors suggest that admissions counselors should consider a wide range of abilities, skills, traits, and attitudes in their communications with adult women considering college.

Weinstein's (1981) discussion of admissions practices with regard to adults also focuses on reentry women. A number of her recommendations seem to be applicable to a general audience. In addition to provisional admission, which she regards as a means of dealing with questionable adult academic records, Weinstein (1981) reminds admissions officers judging old high school records to take grade inflation into account. She suggests that adults should be permitted to submit autobiographical statements as an additional supporting document. She also maintains that special admissions programs for disadvantaged students should be equally available to disadvantaged adult applicants. Questions inappropriate for adults should be removed from admissions forms whenever possible. Admissions staff should receive training with regard to the characteristics and information needs of adult applicants. Specific personnel should be assigned to interview and assist adult applicants.

Academic Success and Factors Affecting Persistence

Once admitted, adult students perform as well in college programs as traditional students (Cagiano, Geisler, and Wilcox, 1977; Mishler, Frederick, Hogan, and Woody, 1982). Despite anxiety about studying again and concerns about other role responsibilities, the adults who are able to stay in school appear to compensate as a result of strong motivation. At least one study indicates that adults returning to their studies perform better than they did before interrupting their schooling. Another study that compared 371 traditional-age undergraduates with 214 adult students on locus of control, self-esteem, communication apprehension, and test anxiety (Escott, Semlak, and Comadena, 1987) indicated no difference in level of communication apprehension, while the adults showed higher self-esteem, more internal locus of control, and a lower level of test anxiety. The best predictors of GPA for the adults were self-esteem and test anxiety.

Mishler, Frederick, Hogan, and Woody (1982) also explored the pace of adult student progress toward graduation. Some claim that the higher GPAs of adults are due to the small number of credits taken each semester. The work of Mishler, Frederick, Hogan, and Woody (1982) did not support this idea. These authors examined the number of credits taken each semester, the frequency of stopout, and the proportion of adults who returned to college as "special" students with a small credit load. Transcript analysis that compared the records of 180 adult students with those of 230 younger students indicated that, contrary to common belief, most adult students maintained an almost full-time load. At least 54 percent enrolled for an average of twelve credits per semester; another 44 percent maintained an average of seven to eleven credits per semester. Only 2 percent pursued a degree by taking one or two courses each semester. Adult student records were characterized by greater variability in credit load from semester to semester; thus, their pace was less consistent. However, once they were enrolled, most adults enrolled continuously until graduation. A substantial minority (40 percent) did stop out at least once—but so did 19 percent of the younger students.

Attrition

Despite typically good progress among persisters, adult students have a higher rate of attrition (Bean and Metzner, 1985). Research on attrition among adult students is complicated by the task of distinguishing between dropouts and temporary stopouts. Smith and Sugarman (1984) compared nonpersisters of traditional and nontraditional age in a community and technical college. They found older nonpersisters to be more satisfied with their contacts with teachers, more likely to have attended school in the evening, more likely to live in the same county as the institution, and more likely to have a lower high school average than younger nonpersisters. However, the operational definition of nonpersistence used in this study is questionable: All students enrolled in the selected fall semester who did not enroll in the following spring were identified as nonpersisters. Weidman (1985) has reported research among adult students at a four-year university that aimed at identifying variables distinguishing persisters from nonpersisters. Four variables were found to be most predictive of persistence: having financial aid, going to school full-time, age (persisters were younger), and GPA (persisters had higher GPAs). Weidman (1985) sees such research as offering promise that we can build a model of adult student persistence.

Bean and Metzner (1985) conducted a comprehensive review of the literature in an effort to build such a model. They reviewed studies of attrition among both traditional and nontraditional undergraduate students as well as descriptive literature on nontraditional students. While they included enrollment status (part-time), age (twenty-five or older), and residence status (commuting) in their definition of *nontraditional,* they report the limited research on factors related to attrition of adult students separately. Their attrition model, said to be modified significantly from one developed to explain attrition among traditional undergraduates, includes four sets of variables: The defining and background variables include age, enrollment status (part-time or full-time), residence status, educational goals, high school academic performance, ethnicity, and sex. The academic variables include study skills and habits, academic advising, absenteeism, certainty with regard to major, and course availability. The environmental variables include finances, hours of employment, outside encouragement, family responsibility, opportunity to transfer, and social integration. The academic outcomes include GPA and such "psychological" outcomes as perceived utility of degree, satisfaction with student role, level of goal commitment, stress, and intent to leave.

Two aspects of their discussion are important here. The first is their presumption that social integration, which in their view is related to interaction with faculty and peers on campus, is likely to have a much less significant relationship to attrition for nontraditional students than previous undergraduate attrition models have assumed. They emphasize the importance of external environmental factors for adult and commuter students, including such influences as family responsibility and encouragement from family and employers. The second aspect is their discussion of compensatory interactions. They believe that external variables are so important for nontraditional students that negative environmental variables can outweigh equivalent positive academic variables. For instance, problems with childcare or work schedules can lead to dropout even for students who have good study habits and adequate academic support. They also hypothesize an interaction between academic and psychological outcomes. Accordingly, a high perception of the utility of the degree may counteract a low GPA, while a student with an adequate GPA may drop out if pursuit of the degree is not seen as bringing progress toward a desired goal. The second compensatory effect would explain the mysterious dropouts of high-achieving adult students. The first compensatory effect poses more problems for the institution, since most environmental variables are not under its control. Bean and Metzner (1985, p. 494) conclude that "for nontraditional students, environmental support compensates for weak academic support, but academic support will not compensate for weak environmental support."

Institutional Responses to Retain Adult Students

Although we have relatively little definitive information about the influences on adult student persistence, a number of institutional responses have been developed in an attempt to meet the needs of adult students and promote their academic success. I will emphasize the practices that can be implemented within traditional degree programs. The reader who is interested in alternative and nontraditional programs for adults will be impressed by the programs listed by de la Croix de la Fayette (1984), which include nonresidential degree programs, independent study programs, external degree programs, programs without a campus, correspondence schools, and degree programs that can be completed on weekends or by the use of media. I will also emphasize modifications of curriculum, academic support, and student services. Needless to say, the availability of all university services at hours convenient to adult students is an institutionwide policy that reflects institutional commitment to lifelong learning.

Preadmission Programs. A number of institutions offer workshops or courses intended for adults considering a return to higher education. Smith and Regan (1983) found that most of the adults who came to a life-reassessment course were seeking new opportunities or goals. Relatively few were looking for reinforcement for support in reentry. Yet, in retrospect the support that they obtained for reentry was valuable to at least 25 percent of the participants. Within one year after the course, 55 percent had enrolled in college, and 14 percent had sought new employment. Of those who took jobs, 30 percent had enrolled in college by the time of a follow-up three to six years later.

Special Scheduling and Locations. One way of supporting adult students is by making courses available to them during convenient evening and weekend hours. Thompson (1985) describes a variety of scheduling patterns that colleges around the country have found to be effective. Local research is probably the best way of finding out the most desired times for the adult students whom you think will be interested in your particular academic program. Institutions with downtown centers, including Johns Hopkins, the University of Wisconsin–Milwaukee, and the University of New Orleans, have brought the courses to the students ("Downtown Centers," 1987). On-site degree programs offered at the workplace are an increasingly common variation on this theme, although Rodgers (1986) stresses the importance of the role of the program coordinator in preventing and correcting misperceptions that develop as a result of two very different orientations to the same program.

Orientation Program. Activities ranging from the half-day workshop to the full-semester course have been used to introduce adult students to campus resources. Study skills instruction and life-planning exercises are often incorporated into orientation programs of longer duration. The most extensive orientation is offered through courses resembling the typical freshman seminar course that have been designed with adult needs in mind. A number of institutions, including Empire State College, Penn State University, University of Maryland, and Widener University, offer courses of this type. The Empire State College course includes sections on adult learning and development and the purposes of higher education (Steltenpohl and Shipton, 1986), as does the course at Penn State.

Special Sections. At the University of South Carolina and other institutions, adult students begin in a transition program in which specially selected instructors offer designated sections of regular academic courses (Fidler, 1986).

Academic Advising. At some institutions, specially trained advisers are designated to work with adult students. For institutions where adult advisers are not available, Bitterman (1985) suggests training for faculty advisers and regular advising staff aimed at developing the needed counseling and interviewing skills as well the awareness that is critical to effective work with adult advisees.

Remediation. Like younger students, some adults have specific skills deficits. The effectiveness of study skills instruction has been demonstrated with adult students (Tyson and Sy, 1977). High-risk adults may profit from remediation even more than high-risk students of traditional age (Clarke, 1982).

Support Groups. Many campuses have support groups for adult students. These groups have names like Students Older Than Average. While many adults choose not to become involved in such organizations, they do offer a critical form of support for those who need it. White (1984) stresses the importance of effective leadership, clarity of purpose, careful scheduling, widespread promotion, and institutional recognition for the success of such groups. It is important for student leaders and faculty or staff advisers not to become discouraged by the sporadic patterns of participation that often appear. The adult student's busy life schedule, not disinterest, is often the explanation for such patterns.

Special Programs. Some unique programs aimed at meeting the needs of adult students have been developed within the framework of otherwise traditional programs. The Experiential Learning Program at Ohio University (Mark and DeWees, 1984) includes a credit course on portfolio development. The Family Life Education program at Wright State University (Phillipp, 1986) provides teaching experience for Wright State students while offering courses for the school-age children of adult students. Plans include learning experiences to be shared by the whole family. Life experience in community action has served as the usual beginning point for the minority females who have been the primary participants in the Public Policy program at Saint Peter's College in New Jersey (Surrey and Perry, 1986).

Summary

Demographic patterns indicate that adult students are likely to remain a significant portion of the student body in higher education at least until the turn of the century. This chapter has addressed a number of issues related to the recruitment, admissions, and academic success of adult students, and it has presented a variety of institutional practices aimed at retention of adult students. At least four priorities for further research and program development emerge, one suggested by its presence in the literature and three by their absence.

The model of adult attrition that Bean and Metzner (1985) have proposed reminds us that, even as we develop programs aimed at retaining adult students, we know surprisingly little about the factors that influence persistence among the members of this group. And, we know almost nothing about the characteristics and needs of certain segments of the adult student population, including minority adults. Yet, demographics suggest that American society will be increasingly comprised of ethnic minorities, for whom the rate of participation in higher education has been higher in recent decades at ages over twenty-five than it has at traditional ages. We cannot begin to plan programs aimed at meeting the needs of these adults unless we have more information. Similarly, it is important that we begin to investigate the outcomes of participation in higher education at a later age. Do adults achieve the goals that lead them to return to school? Finally, in-service programs for faculty and staff are needed to foster a more comprehensive approach to meeting the needs of adult students than direct interventions with students alone can provide.

References

Apps, J. *The Adult Learner on Campus: A Guide for Instructors and Administrators.* New York: Cambridge Books, 1981.

Aslanian, C. B., and Brickell, H. M. *Americans in Transition: Life Changes as Reasons for Adult Learning.* New York: College Entrance Examination Board, 1980.

Bean, J. P., and Metzner, B. S. "A Conceptual Model of Nontraditional Undergraduate Student Attrition." *Review of Educational Research*, 1985, 55 (4), 484-540.

Bishop, J., and Van Dyk, J. "Can Adults Be Hooked on College? Some Determinants of Adult College Attendance." *Journal of Higher Education*, 1977, 48 (1), 39-63.

Bitterman, J. "Academic Advising and Adult Education: An Emerging Synthesis." *NACADA Journal*, 1985, 5 (2), 29-33.

Cagiano, A., Geisler, M., and Wilcox, L. "The Academic Performance of Returning Adult Students." *College Board Review*, 1977, 106, 13-16.

Campbell, J. F., and Spiro, L. M. "Evaluation of the Impact of Media Marketing Strategies on Continuing Education Enrollments." Paper presented at the annual forum of the Association for Institutional Research, Denver, May 1982.

Clarke, J. H. "The Effectiveness of Remediation Among High-Risk College Freshmen of Different Ages." 1982. (ED 227 727)

Cotten, C. C., and Stock, W. P. "Alternative Admissions for Adult Students at California State University, Fresno." *College and University*, 1985, 60, 229-241.

de la Croix de la Fayette, J-M. *Directory of United States Traditional and Alternative Colleges and Universities.* Washington, D.C.: National Association of State Approved Colleges and Universities, 1984.

"Downtown Centers Meet Working Adults' Needs with Flexible, Convenient, and Practical Programming." *NUCEA News*, 1987, 3 (8), 4-5.

Escott, M. D., Semlak, W. D., and Comadena, M. E. "Text Anxiety, Locus of Control, and Self-Esteem as Predictors of Achievement: A Comparative Study of Traditional Students and Adult Learners." Paper presented at the annual NUCEA Region IV Conference, Columbus, Ohio, October 1987.

Fidler, D. S. "Attracting and Retaining Adult Students: Mature Students' Program and Weekend Program." In *Proceedings of the National Conference on the Adult Learner.* Columbia: University of South Carolina, 1986.

Gallien, K. J. "For Adult Audiences Only." *Currents*, 1986, 12 (5), 16-20.

Hexter, H., and Andersen, C. J. *Admission and Credit Policies for Adult Learners.* Higher Education Panel Report No. 72. Washington, D.C.: American Council on Education, 1986.

Hirsh, J. B. *Proceedings of the National Conferences on the Adult Learner.* Columbia: University of South Carolina, 1986.

Hodgkinson, H. L. "Guess Who's Coming to College? A Demographic Portrait of Students in the 1990s." *Academe,* 1983, *69* (2), 13-20.

Magarell, J. "The Enrollment Boom Among Older Americans: One in Three College Students Is Now Over Twenty-Five Years Old." *The Chronicle of Higher Education,* May 4, 1981, p. 3.

Mark, M., and DeWees, P. "Recruitment, Retention, and Alumni Development of Adult Learners Through Assessment of Prior Learning." *Lifelong Learning: An Omnibus of Research and Practice,* 1984, *8* (1), 18-20.

Mishler, C., Frederick, D., Hogan, T. P., and Woody, S. "Adult Students' Pace Toward Graduation." *College and University,* 1982, *57* (1), 31-41.

"More Institutional Recruitment Efforts and Dollars Specifically Targeted at Potential Adult and Part-Time Students." *NUCEA News,* 1987, *3* (3), 3.

Murphy, D. T., and Achtziger, M. A. "Recruiting the Older, Adult, Female Student." *College and University,* 1982, *57* (3), 314-322.

O'Connor, K., and Aasheim, I. J. "Working with Nontraditional Students: Women in Transition." Paper presented at the Regional Conference on University Teaching, Las Cruces, New Mexico, Jan. 1985. (ED 253 184)

Phillipp, J. "Family Life Education: An Innovative Educational Program for Adult Students' Families." In *Proceedings of the National Conference on the Adult Learner.* Columbia: University of South Carolina, 1986.

Pitt Community College. *A Model for Recruiting the New Community College Student.* Greenville, N.C.: Pitt Community College, 1985. (ED 267 187)

Rodgers, M. "Implementing Off-Campus Credit Programs." In *Proceedings of the National Conference on the Adult Learner.* Columbia: University of South Carolina, 1986.

Ross, J. M. "Transitions, Triggers, and the Return to College: No Simple Decision." *Journal of College Student Development,* 1988, *29* (2), 112-118.

Sewall, T. "A Study of Adult Undergraduates: What Causes Them to Seek a Degree?" *Journal of College Student Personnel,* 1984, *25,* 309-314.

Smith, A. D., and Sugarman, M. N. "Nontraditional and Traditional Student Persisters and Nonpersisters in the Community and Technical College." *NACADA Journal,* 1984, *4,* 47-57.

Smith, J. W., and Regan, M. C. "A Longitudinal Evaluation of Life Reassessment Courses." *Journal of College Student Personnel,* 1983, *24* (3), 231-235.

Steltenpohl, E., and Shipton, J. "Facilitating a Successful Transition to College for Adults." *Journal of Higher Education,* 1986, *56* (6), 637-658.

Surrey, D., and Perry, R. "Urban, Poor, Female and Returning to School: Providing for the Advantaged Urban Adult." In *Proceedings of the National Conference on the Adult Learner.* Columbia: University of South Carolina, 1986.

Thieman, T., and Marsh-Williams, P. "Prediction of Academic Performance of Adult Women in a Weekend College Program." *Journal of College Student Personnel,* 1984, *25,* 260-264.

Thompson, H. L. "The Ready for Prime-Time Players: Colleges Cater to the Adult Schedule." *Educational Record,* 1985, *66* (3), 33-37.

Tyson, C. S., and Sy, M. J. "The Effectiveness of Study Skills Instruction with Students in an Adult Degree Program." *Journal of College Student Personnel,* 1977, *18,* 478-481.

Weidman, J. C. "Retention of Nontraditional Students in Postsecondary Education." Paper presented at the annual meeting of the American Educational Research Association, Chicago, April 1985.

Weinstein, L. *Recruitment and Admissions: Opening the Door for Reentry Women. Field Evaluation Draft.* Washington, D.C.: Women's Educational Equity Act Program, 1981.

White, C. J. "Adult Student Support Groups on the Campus." *NASPA Journal,* Fall 1984, pp. 54-59.

Wisconsin Assessment Center. *The Adult Student. Research Findings from the Wisconsin Assessment Center.* Green Bay: University of Wisconsin, 1983. (ED 241 733)

Jovita Martin Ross is assistant professor in the Adult Education Program at Pennsylvania State University, University Park, Pennsylvania.

Recruitment and retention strategies in continuing higher education must consider both organizational and programmatic approaches and focus on the subtleties of learners' participation patterns.

Recruiting and Retaining Adult Students in Continuing Higher Education

Joe F. Donaldson

Continuing higher education (CHE) has both functional and organizational dimensions. CHE is defined as continuing education programming for adults sponsored by institutions of higher education that is operated outside mainstream campus programming (Talbert, 1987). It includes correspondence and other forms of individualized study; a variety of noncredit learning experiences, including conferences, workshops, and courses; and credit courses and degree programs at all levels. The specific organizational arrangement for CHE varies by institution, but it is generally characterized by campus or academic units that act as interfaces between academic units and adult client groups. The diversity of CHE programs, clients, and organizations requires us to focus on some overarching concepts related to recruitment and retention. Consequently, the discussion that follows takes all types of CHE programming for groups of adults into account and considers recruitment and retention from both organizational and programming perspectives.

P. S. Cookson (ed.). *Recruiting and Retaining Adult Students.*
New Directions for Continuing Education, no. 41. San Francisco: Jossey-Bass, Spring 1989.

Participants in Continuing Higher Education

What do we know about the participants in continuing higher education? A profile by Freedman (1987) of participants in programs at four-year colleges and universities provides some answers. Participants range in age from the mid-twenties through retirement years; the largest numbers are between twenty-five and thirty-nine. Approximately three-fourths have full-time jobs, the majority in professional and managerial positions. Almost 79 percent have been in their current position for less than ten years. From the national perspective, their educational experience is more extensive than that of participants in all adult and continuing education programs. In fact, the single most significant predictor of participation in continuing higher education is formal educational attainment.

Slightly more than 50 percent of participants are women. However, the distribution varies significantly with subject area. For example, men predominate in business and engineering programs, while women constitute the overwhelming majority in liberal arts programs. These patterns are beginning to change as increasing numbers of women move into fields traditionally dominated by men. The average family income is well above the national average. However, slightly more than a third are in the lower-middle income bracket and not usually in occupations that receive employer tuition benefits. Most participants are Caucasian. The number of participants of Asian origin is increasing rapidly. Blacks, Hispanics, and Native Americans are grossly underrepresented.

This profile identifies those who are being served and provides some information about the populations to which recruitment efforts can be targeted. It also provides information about the populations for which new programs and new recruiting methods need to be developed if the participants in continuing higher education are to become more culturally and socioeconomically diverse.

The reasons for adults' participation and persistence in continuing higher education are multifaceted and complex, since they are a function of the interaction among personal, situational, and institutional factors. Building on one categorization of adult participants in higher education (Pappas and Loring, 1985), we can divide participants into three broad categories: credential seekers or persons who seek degrees or certificates or who fulfill continuing education participation requirements in order to maintain their credentials; problem solvers—persons who participate in CHE programs to help them solve problems that they face in their jobs or personal lives; and leisure, personal skills, and cultural enrichment seekers—persons who participate in order to enrich themselves, increase their repertoire of personal skills, and spend some part of their leisure time in educational pursuits.

Dimensions of the Program/Participant Transaction

Nevertheless, general profiles and broad categorizations fall far short of describing the dynamic interface between programs and participants. Recruitment and retention in comprehensive continuing education programs require attention to and an understanding of the complexities of this interface. They require attention to both longitudinal and cross-sectional patterns of participation (Pappas and Loring, 1985). They also require a recognition that some unique dimensions arise from the transactions between certain program characteristics and patterns of participation. Four dimensions of the program/participant transaction are to be considered here: the social context of programming, the social organization of potential participants, program continuity, and the social composition of participants. Each dimension delineates an important characteristic of the interface between programming and participation; each has implications for recruitment and retention.

Social Context. Continuing higher education programs occur most often within two social contexts: the individual setting and the collective or group context. In individual setting, individual learners have little interaction with others (Nowlen, 1980). Moore considers recruitment and retention of adult learners in this context in Chapter Eight. This chapter focuses on the collective or group context.

Social Organization. The social organization of potential participants is a measure of their geographic dispersal and the level of social organization among them prior to program participation. The extremes of both dimensions have been labeled *random* and *clustered* (Emery and Trist, 1965). When considered together, these two dimensions form four quadrants divided by two intersecting axes. The geographic dispersion of potential participants ranges from the random scattering of participants throughout a CHE unit's service area to a dense concentration or clustering of participants at specific locations. When social organization is random, individual participants have had few if any previous contacts with one another. When social organization is clustered, participants have had many contacts.

Some examples will help to illustrate these concepts. Programs offered on an open-enrollment basis to the general public at a specific location (for example, a lecture series in the arts offered to persons who live within a twenty-five-mile radius) are offered for potential participants whose social organization is random but whose geographic distribution is relatively clustered. A program offered on a contractual basis for employees of a local company is offered for potential participants whose social organization and geographic distribution are clustered. Members of the organization participate in the program, and their prior and subsequent relationships have a major influence on it (Nowlen, 1980). Participation in the national conferences of professional associations by members who have infrequent telephone and personal contacts between conferences characterize the program offered for participants whose geographic distribution is fairly random but whose social organization falls somewhere between the random and the clustered extremes.

Program Continuity. Programs can range from loosely to tightly coupled (Weick, 1976). In the context of CHE, a loosely coupled program is a single offering that has no curricular relationship with any other offering of the institution. In the tightly coupled program, each individual program is a component of some larger programmatic whole to which it contributes. For example, a series of conferences on different aspects of marketing is more tightly than loosely coupled. Programs can also be even more tightly coupled through sequencing. In this case, each program contributes to the whole, but, in addition, the learning obtained in one program becomes a prerequisite for enrollment in another program.

Sequenced programs can be further characterized by the degree to which participants enter and proceed through the program as a cohort. At one extreme, an entire cohort enters a program and proceeds in lockstep fashion to program completion. At the other extreme, small groups of students enter a program at various times throughout the program cycle and have little contact with one another due to their dispersal among several program offerings.

Social Composition. The term *social composition of participants* refers to the presence or absence of group members who can teach new recruits about the program setting (Wheeler, 1966). When social composition is serial, the group's members include persons who have previously entered a program and from whom new recruits can learn about the program. When social composition is disjunctive, group membership does not include experienced participants. Social composition can be disjunctive both in a loosely coupled program, such as an isolated conference or a single credit course, and in a tightly coupled program in which a single cohort of participants proceeds in lockstep fashion from program entry to exit.

The definitions of these four dimensions of program/participation transaction are somewhat arbitrary. For example, the fact that none of the participants in a program have experienced the program before does not prevent a new recruit from seeking information from others who have attended the program in the past (Wheeler, 1966). Also, each dimension is more properly considered as a continuum than as a dichotomy. For example, programs can vary in their level of coupling, and the social organization of potential participants can range from random to tightly clustered. But, despite these conceptual imperfections, the dimensions, taken together, help to identify some subtle but important factors that can inform recruitment and retention efforts. I will use all four dimensions in the discussion of these two functions that follows.

Recruitment

The recruitment and the retention of learners are interrelated processes, and the effectiveness of the recruitment process, whether it is organizational or programmatic in origin, sets the tone for retention efforts. Recruitment should be a well-developed process that fosters communication between the CHE unit and potential participants. It should also use both organizational and programmatic approaches. Therefore, before we move to a consideration of some specifics of the recruitment process, we need to review two organizational perspectives on recruitment.

Organizational Perspectives on Recruitment. Two strategies that derive from different theories of organizations have relevance for recruitment. The first is an adaptive strategy that has its roots in the resource-dependence models of open-systems theory (Thompson, 1967). The other is an interpretive strategy that has developed from recent research on organizational cultures (Chaffee, 1984, 1985).

Adaptive Strategy. Malaney (1985) used the resource-dependence theory developed by Thompson (1967) to analyze graduate student recruitment among institutions of higher education. Such an analysis is equally applicable to continuing higher education.

For Thompson (1967), administrative action is critically important to the survival of organizations, because they depend on resources found in their environments. Domain is another important issue. An organization's domain includes the claims that it makes for the range of products that it offers, the populations that it serves, and the services that it renders. Unless the continuing higher education unit is totally divorced from the parent institution, its range of programs and thus the client groups that it can serve depend in large part on the domain of its parent institution.

An organization's task environment is its immediate operating environment, which includes individuals, groups, and organizations with which it has direct contact and transactions (Thompson, 1967). In the context of participant recruitment, the task environment consists of customers or potential participants; suppliers of participants, including the general public and organizations, such as business, government, and professional associations; competitors, including other higher education institutions, business and industry, and private continuing education providers; and regulatory groups or organizations whose policies affect recruitment by CHE units (Thompson, 1967). Regulatory groups include state coordinating boards, national and state governmental bodies, professional associations, regional and academic accrediting bodies, and the parent institution itself, whose policies, rules, and procedures submit CHE unit programming and operations to demands and constraints (Knox, 1981).

Exchange forms the basis of the relationship between the organization and potential participants in the task environment (Thompson, 1967). Participants will be willing to exchange their time, money, and energy only if they judge that the organization offers programs of value. The fact that cost (in terms of lack of peer support, time, money, and tuition support) and perceived lack of benefit have been found to deter participation in continuing education (Scanlan and Darkenwald, 1984) supports this view of recruitment as an exchange relationship.

Thompson (1967) identifies two kinds of strategies that organizations use in dealing with their task environments: competitive strategies and cooperative strategies. Competitive strategies include developing alternative sources of needed resources and acquiring a positive and prestigious organizational image (Thompson, 1967; Malaney, 1985). Application of the first competitive strategy to recruitment suggests that continuing educators should consider, first, increasing the variability both of the programs that they offer and of the adult groups that they serve; second, developing relationships with multiple suppliers of participants so that additional numbers of participants who are geographically or socially clustered can be recruited; and, third, exploring ways of expanding the unit's service area to include the new potential participants who are scattered or clustered throughout the new regions. It also means that, as our society becomes more culturally pluralistic, CHE units will have to become informed about and develop relationships with "suppliers" of potential participants who are socially and culturally organized in ways that continuing education practitioners do not understand or appreciate.

Application of the second competitive strategy to recruitment suggests that continuing educators need to take the image of their parent institution into account when they develop recruitment strategies. The academic reputations of some institutions naturally help to attract participants. The reputations that other institutions have for excellent instruction or service to adults are also aids in recruitment. But, if potential learners do not view either the institution's or the CHE unit's reputation as positive, recruitment will suffer. A positive reputational image is built in large part on participants' perception of program quality and excellence, the perceived lack of which has been found to deter participation (Scanlan and Darkenwald, 1984). The application of this organizational strategy requires continuing educators to attend to quality in programs, instruction, marketing, and dealings with potential participants so that a positive reputation can be fostered.

Thompson (1967) identifies three cooperative strategies: contracting, coalescing, and coopting. CHE units can contract with suppliers of participants—business and industry, government, school districts, nonprofit organizations, and professional associations—to provide programs to members of these organizations. Contracting taps socially clustered groups of participants and reduces the costs of marketing, since programs are marketed to organizations rather than to individuals.

Coalescing involves developing a joint venture with other organizations in the unit's task environment and coordinating organizational activities (Beder, 1984). Coalitions can be developed with competitors and noncompetitors alike. When coalitions are formed with competitors, they can have the effect of decreasing harmful competition. They can also help to extend the unit's domain, thereby adding to the organization's array of potential participants (Beder, 1984).

Coopting is the process of absorbing new elements into the organization (Thompson, 1967). Application of this strategy includes cosponsorship of programs (Beder, 1984), appointment of representatives from suppliers to advisory committees, and the use of adjunct instructors provided by suppliers in program development and instruction (Malaney, 1985). Each application is aimed at developing and building relationships that help to strengthen links with pools of potential participants. These relationships also facilitate communication with potential participants by giving CHE units access to mailing lists and in-house publications.

Interpretive Strategy. Although the interpretive strategy is not as fully developed as the adaptive strategy, it, too, has relevance for recruitment. Interpretive strategy is based on two central assumptions about organizational life: the concept of social contract and the concept of socially constructed reality. The concept of social contract depicts an organization as a collection of cooperative agreements entered into by individuals on their own volition (Chaffee, 1985). The concept of social contract is very appropriate to the phenomenon of participation in continuing education, given the voluntary nature of most participation and the fact that through the registration process individuals and the organization enter into a contract—for the provision of service by the organization and for participation by the individual. Exchange is also important, since the organization's survival depends on its ability to recruit enough individuals to cooperate in mutually beneficial exchange relationships (Chaffee, 1985).

The concept of socially constructed reality holds that reality and meaning are developed through social interchange or communication. The purpose of communication is to help organizational stakeholders understand the organization and what it stands for (Chaffee, 1985). The goal of interpretive strategy is to develop metaphors or frames of reference that guide individual perceptions and attitudes about the organization in an effort to achieve organizational legitimacy. It calls for symbol development and for the improvement of relationships and interactions among organizational participants and potential participants (Chaffee, 1985).

Interpretive strategy has several implications for continuing higher education. First, it draws attention to the importance of communication and language. Although lack of information about programs has been identified as a barrier to participation (Darkenwald and Merriam, 1982), interpretive strategy says that information alone is insufficient. Instead, it calls for use of language in promotion that helps to develop perceptions of programs that develops human connectedness, and that communicates to potential participants that the institution cares about them. Second, interpretive strategy calls for the use of symbols. Although each symbol must also have substance, the creation of advisory and program-planning committees, the scheduling of informational meetings for potential participants, and hassle-free registration procedures all have symbolic value in that they all communicate the unit's commitment to the individual who participates in its programs. Finally, interpretive strategy calls for attention to the human element in developing and maintaining relationships with others outside the CHE unit.

Research on the strategic management of small private colleges (Chaffee, 1984) found that the most resilient institutions (including those that opened their doors to adult learners) used both adaptive and interpretive strategies. Thus, interpretive strategy can build on and extend the use of adaptive strategies for recruitment.

Programming Perspectives on Recruitment. An organizational perspective on recruitment sets the context for recruitment efforts tied specifically to programming. Much has been written about marketing and promotional techniques that can be used in successful continuing education recruitment efforts (Beder, 1986). Rather than cover ground that has been well trod by others, I will discuss the implications that program continuity, participation patterns, and program packaging have for recruitment.

Trajectory Theory. The term *trajectory theory* refers to an assumption often made within continuing higher education that noncredit courses serve as a recruitment tool for credit courses and degree programs. Noncredit courses are viewed as offering nonthreatening situations in which adults who are anxious about reentry can test the academic waters (Campbell, Hentschel, Rossi, and Spiro, 1984).

Research on the trajectory theory has been limited, and the results are mixed. One study of participants at a suburban community education center served by four continuing education providers found that only 10 percent of the degree and 15 percent of the nondegree students had first enrolled in noncredit courses (Campbell, Hentschel, Rossi, and Spiro, 1984). The investigators concluded from their data that the trajectory theory was unfounded. In contrast, Willett (1982) found that 49 percent of the persisters (26 percent of the total cohort) in the continuing education program of a two-year college went on to take a credit course (58 percent in the first or second semester after their first enrollment).

It is likely that the differences in the findings of these two studies were due in part to differences in program continuity. The odds are that the noncredit and credit programs of the two-year college were more tightly coupled than the programs offered at the off-campus center. Campbell, Hentschel, Rossi, and Spiro (1984, pp. 16-17) recognized the lack of coupling between noncredit courses and degree programs at the off-campus center and concluded that "consciously developed curricular linkages between noncredit courses and degree programs and creative marketing strategies . . . could create the bridge which is currently lacking." The remarkable similarity in the frequency with which noncredit and credit degree students reported job-related reasons for enrollment provided further support for their conclusion. In accord with their recommendations, the institution where they worked tightened the coupling between its noncredit and credit degree programs. Preliminary reports suggest that the college has been successful in helping adults to move from noncredit courses to credit programs (Campbell, Hentschel, and Spiro, 1986). Thus, the trajectory theory seems to have potential for program recruitment. But, it can work only if the subtleties of participation patterns and program continuity are understood and if programming and marketing are adapted to help participants to move from one form of participation to another.

Packaging. The packaging of programs or tightening the linkages among separate offerings can also help recruitment efforts. Here too, the subtleties of participation patterns must be understood. Degree seekers (Pappas and Loring, 1985) are the most loyal participants in continuing higher education. Their recruitment results in repeat enrollments leading to the degrees that they pursue. In contrast, nondegree credit students appear to be the least loyal participants (Campbell, Hentschel, Rossi, and Spiro, 1984). Their participation is sporadic, and they bring a consumer orientation to participation (Campbell, Hentschel, Rossi, and Spiro, 1984). Their reasons for enrollment put them in both the credential-seeking and the problem-solving categories of participants in CHE. However, the enrollment patterns of these participants do not mean that programs cannot be packaged to help recruit them. For example, the University of Illinois at Urbana-Champaign has identified off-campus programming locations where a series of related agriculture credit courses are offered to meet specific regional needs. Although these programs do not lead to degrees or certificates, they are more conducive to an effective and focused recruitment effort than multiple and scattered offerings of single, unrelated courses.

It is also possible to package noncredit programs so as to consider different aspects of a single topic. Such packages provide a focused recruitment effort for persons who participate primarily in order to solve problems or improve their personal skills. The possibility of packaging programs for persons who seek cultural enrichment should also not be overlooked. Such a recruitment strategy has been found to be particularly successful for noncredit programming in the arts (Donaldson and Perrino, 1981). Packaging provides another example of how recruitment practices can enhance retention. It provides a means of focusing recruitment efforts, but it also fosters repeat enrollments—a longitudinal measure of retention of participants in the programs offered by a CHE unit.

Retention

The literature suggests that we can expect persons to complete programs if they have succeeded in past educational endeavors, if they are not anxious about returning to sponsored learning, and—in the case of credit programs—if they have relatively high ability (Pappas and Loring, 1985). Persistence has also been said to be a function of situational or environmental factors, which include finances or financial support, hours of employment, outside encouragement, and family responsibilities (Bean and Metzner, 1985). Several variables that continuing educators and instructors can control to varying degrees have been found to enhance persistence. These variables include clear communication about the availability and nature of programs; programming that addresses the expectations and needs of learners and that is relevant to their lives; strong student support services, especially in the area of financial aid; and tailor-made and time-compressed programs (Pappas and Loring, 1985).

The identification of factors that enhance persistence has come primarily from the literature that addresses the retention of adults who have returned to seek degrees, especially undergraduate degrees. With the exception of learner persistence in correspondence study, the topic of participant retention has received little attention for other CHE program areas. This neglect has two sources. First, with the exception of degree seekers, adult participation in CHE programs is sporadic, and turnover from one academic term or program to another is high. As a result Pappas and Loring (1985) suggest that a cross-sectional (rather than a longitudinal) perspective on persistence is most appropriate for learners who are not seeking degrees. The major retention strategy recommended for this group of participants is to develop programs and counseling services so excellent that the resulting good experiences will encourage learners to enroll again in the institution's programs. Second, the energy spent on retention efforts for the many short-term programs offered for noncredit and nondegree participants appears to be ill spent in view of the level of resources that need to be spent in order to develop excellent programs and recruit participants.

However, CHE needs a broader view of retention than the one just described. This broader view would focus, first, on the use of both longitudinal and cross-sectional perspectives; second, on managing the meaning of participation; third, on the development of communities of learners.

Longitudinal and Cross-Sectional Perspectives. The broader view just advocated would first consider retention from both longitudinal and cross-sectional perspectives and would take into account the subtleties of participation patterns in the full array of a CHE unit's programs. Of course, degree programming requires a longitudinal perspective. But, the few longitudinal studies that have been conducted on noncredit enrollment patterns indicate that noncredit students show more institutional loyalty over time than people might have assumed (Willett, 1982; Campbell, Hentschel, Rossi, and Spiro, 1984). And, as noted earlier, the packaging of programs can promote longitudinal retention in an institution's credit and noncredit programs. Thus, a broad view of retention is important because it is part of a longitudinal feedback loop that has important implications both for recruitment and for retention in continuing education programs.

To gain a longitudinal perspective on retention, studies that track student flow through CHE programs over time will be needed. The success that Brockport College had in using a longitudinal perspective in reviewing and revising its recruitment and retention strategies provides evidence of the benefits that such an approach can have (Campbell, Hentschel, and Spiro, 1986). Longitudinal student-tracking systems are now being developed for traditional credit programming to support enrollment management, local planning, and decision making. Continuing higher education can develop and use similar systems.

Managing Meaning. The broad view of retention advocated here would also explore the role that the management of meaning has in retaining participants. An interpretive strategy and social contract approach to retention would identify some factors that were worthy of exploration. As noted earlier, the social contract approach emphasizes social interchange as a means of developing shared meaning and human connectedness. Communications with program participants can also be used to develop this shared meaning and increase attachment. Rites and rituals can also serve symbolic purposes in this type of communication. For example, a large midwestern research university has an excellence in off-campus teaching award program. As part of the selection process, students receive letters asking them to nominate faculty members for the award. This letter not only has a substantive purpose, but it also has a symbolic function. It informs students that the institution cares about exemplary instruction for adults and that it cares about the instruction that each student is receiving (Donaldson, 1988).

Interpretive strategy and the concept of the social contract have only recently gained prominence in the study of organizations and their activities. Therefore, much remains to be learned about the specifics of their application and effect. However, it is already clear that administrators should attend to the management of meaning and human connectedness through communications. The use of language and symbols can become useful tools in retaining learners if we recognize their importance and explore the ways in which they support learner persistence.

Developing a Community of Learners. Finally, the concept of social integration needs to be explored and refined in the broad view of retention that is recommended here. The term *social integration* refers to the level and quality of interactions among learners and instructors and to the social and academic support that participants provide to each other. To date, the definition of social integration remains grounded in the framework of traditional college attendance; as a result, it has been held to have little if any influence on retention (Bean and Metzner, 1985). Yet, adult students do interact with others within program contexts, but the form of their interaction differs considerably from that described for full-time college students. Continuing educators need to consider some alternative program configurations that can facilitate social integration. Some alternate but subtle ways in which social integration can be manifest and further developed in continuing higher education are suggested in the paragraphs that follow.

There is some evidence that communities of learners can be developed within CHE programs. These communities are characterized by intense involvement, cohesiveness, a focus on common goals, full participation, caring, sharing, and helping. If the educational experience lasts long enough, the community can be developed within the context of a single offering, whether credit or noncredit. It is the kind of community that Collins (1985) had in mind when he described short-term residential conferences. The factor is important for adult learners. For example, the fostering of a community of learners has been found to be one characteristic that adult students include in their descriptions of exemplary instructors (Donaldson, 1988). However, the development of a community of learners within a single offering cannot be left to chance. It requires program instructors or facilitators to support its development so that programs will not only be relevant and well taught but will also include dimensions of community.

A community of learners can also be developed among participants of packaged programs. Doing so requires program planning that takes into account the social composition of participants, their prior social organization, and the ways in which these two dimensions of program/participant transaction interact within a program. The next three paragraphs examine the importance of including these dimensions and their interaction in planning. The discussion is most applicable to programming that is tightly coupled, such as degree and certificate programs, credit course sequences, workshop series, and sequences of noncredit courses, but it illustrates what can be done in other programming contexts.

A cohort of adult students that proceeds in lockstep fashion through a program seems to provide a social composition more amenable to the development of community than a serial social composition. Over time, participants get to know one another and instructors very well, and the quality of these relationships should facilitate the development of community. In addition, a clustered social organization (for example, people who work in the same company or for the same school district) should strengthen the community-building process in cohort programming. Although I am not aware of any research that directly supports this claim, my experience suggests that community building is indeed strengthened when participants have known one another and been in frequent contact before the program begins.

However, cohort programs lack persons who can teach each new group of students about the program setting. Since knowing about the program is important to student persistence, the serial model of social composition has some application to community building. For example, use of experienced students as mentors for new students has been cited as extremely important in reducing attrition (Pappas and Loring, 1985).

Thus, overlapping cohort groups formed among participants whose social organization is clustered seems most able to support the development of a learning community within tightly coupled programs. The combination of a clustered social organization with overlapping cohorts capitalizes on the advantages of each model. Participants know each other and are in frequent contact before and during the program, they proceed through the program together, and they have access to experienced colleagues who can teach them about the program. The interactions of social composition and prior social organization can be ranked as follows for their role in community building among adult learners:

Rank	Social Composition	Social Organization
1	Overlapping cohorts	Clustered
2	Overlapping cohorts	Random
3	Cohort	Clustered
4	Cohort	Random
5	Serial	Clustered
6	Serial	Random

The preceding discussion shows how program planning can use some subtle dimensions of participation to facilitate community building among learners. However, this type of planning can at best provide no more than the basis for a learning community. Community building requires continuing educators and instructors to commit to the development of programs with an integrity that persists over time. Programs must adhere to the schedule and sequencing that has been established and communicated to participants. Information about changes in the program, its policies, or procedures must be communicated in timely ways through newsletters, orientation sessions, counseling, and advisement. And, when possible, efforts must also be made to provide social opportunities that permit participants to get to know one another.

I have suggested that continuing higher education needs to broaden its view of retention. This broadened view would focus on both longitudinal and cross-sectional perspectives of retention and the subtleties of participation patterns, on the ways in which the management of meaning can contribute to retention, and on the ways in which supportive communities can be developed among adult learners. This broadened view must also experiment and explore the effects of these three suggestions. Without continual experimentation and evaluation of these and other ideas in practice, the benefits of retention efforts may never be fully realized.

Summary

This chapter has considered recruitment and retention in continuing higher education from a comprehensive perspective. The comprehensive perspective provides a context within which decisions about specific practices at the programmatic level can be judged.

Recruitment and retention issues cut across the division of CHE programming into credit and noncredit, course and conference, and other categories. We must find ways of assessing the impact that adult participation in different types of CHE programs has on the vitality of the entire CHE operation and its parent institution. Strategies for the two processes have both organizational and programmatic dimensions, and acting on both strengthens recruitment and retention efforts. Understanding issues of recruitment and retention in CHE also requires us to attend to the longitudinal, cross-sectional, and subtle characteristics of participation patterns within all CHE programs. Data collection must keep these characteristics in mind so that support for local program planning and decision making can be improved. The management of meaning and the development of communities of learners have promise for increasing learner retention. All these ideas need to be tested in practice before their full import can be known. Above all else, strengthening recruitment and retention efforts in CHE requires us to look at these processes in new and comprehensive ways so that practice can continue to be improved.

References

Bean, J. P., and Metzner, B. S. "A Conceptual Model of Nontraditional Undergraduate Student Attrition." *Review of Educational Research*, 1985, 55 (4), 485-540.

Beder, H. "Interorganizational Cooperation: Why and How?" In H. Beder (ed.), *Realizing the Potential of Interorganizational Cooperation*. New Directions for Continuing Education, no. 23. San Francisco: Jossey-Bass, 1984.

Beder, H. (ed.). *Marketing Continuing Education*. New Directions for Continuing Education, no. 31. San Francisco: Jossey-Bass, 1986.

Campbell, J. F., Hentschel, D., Rossi, K., and Spiro, L. M. "Examination of Adult Student Participation: Is the Conventional Wisdom Confirmed?" Paper presented at the annual forum of the Association for Institutional Research, Fort Worth, Tex., May 6-9, 1984.

Campbell, J. F., Hentschel, D., and Spiro, L. M. "Studying Participation Patterns of Adult Learners: Relevance to Enrollment Management." In J. A. Lucas (ed.), *AIR Professional File No. 7*. Tallahassee, Fla.: Association for Institutional Research, 1986.

Chaffee, E. E. "Successful Strategic Management in Small Private Colleges." *Journal of Higher Education*, 1984, 55 (2), 211-241.

Chaffee, E. E. "Three Models of Strategy." *Academy of Management Review*, 1985, 10 (1), 89-96.

Collins, M. "Quality Learning Through Residential Colleges." In P. J. Ilsley (ed.), *Improving Conference Design and Outcomes*. New Directions for Continuing Education, no. 28. San Francisco: Jossey-Bass, 1985.

Darkenwald, G. G., and Merriam, S. B. *Adult Education: Foundations of Practice*. New York: Harper & Row, 1982.

Donaldson, J. F. "Exemplary Instruction of Adults: The Case of an Excellence in Off-Campus Teaching Award, Part II." *Journal of Continuing Higher Education*, 1988, 36 (2), 11-18.

Donaldson, J. F., and Perrino, D. "An Integrated Program of Noncredit Lecture/Discussion Series in the Arts." In *Innovations in Continuing Education*. Washington, D.C.: National University Continuing Education Association and The American College Testing Program, 1981.

Emery, F. E., and Trist, E. L. "The Casual Texture of Organizational Environments." *Human Relations*, 1965, 18 (1), 21-32.

Freedman, L. *Quality in Continuing Education: Principles, Practices, and Standards for Colleges and Universities*. San Francisco: Jossey-Bass, 1987.

Knox, A. B. "The Continuing Education Agency and Its Parent Organization." In J. C. Votruba (ed.), *Strengthening Internal Support for Continuing Education*. New Directions for Continuing Education, no. 9. San Francisco: Jossey-Bass, 1981.

Malaney, G. D. "An Organizational Perspective of Graduate Student Recruitment: A Resource-Dependent Approach." *Review of Higher Education*, 1985, 8 (4), 375-386.

Nowlen, P. M. "Program Origins." In A. B. Knox and Associates, *Developing, Administering, and Evaluating Adult Education*. San Francisco: Jossey-Bass, 1980.

Pappas, J. P., and Loring, R. K. "Returning Learners." In L. Noel, R. Levitz, D. Saluri, and Associates, *Increasing Student Retention: Effective Programs and Practices for Reducing the Dropout Rate*. San Francisco: Jossey-Bass, 1985.

Scanlan, C. S., and Darkenwald, G. G. "Identifying Deterrents to Participation in Continuing Education." *Adult Education Quarterly*, 1984, 34 (3), 155-166.

Talbert, K. "Adult and Continuing Education: A Semantic Dilemma." *Lifelong Learning: An Omnibus of Practice and Research*, 1987, *11* (1), 8-9.

Thompson, J. D. *Organizations in Action: Social Science Bases of Administrative Theory.* New York: McGraw-Hill, 1967.

Weick, K. E. "Educational Organizations as Loosely Coupled Systems." *Administrative Science Quarterly*, 1976, *21* (1), 1-19.

Wheeler, S. "The Structure of Formally Organized Socialization Settings." In O. G. Brim, Jr., and S. Wheeler (eds.), *Socialization After Childhood: Two Essays.* New York: Wiley, 1966.

Willett, L. H. "Continuing Education Student Flow Analysis." *Research in Higher Education*, 1982, *17* (2), 155-164.

Joe F. Donaldson is associate professor of adult education at Pennsylvania State University and current chair of the Division of Research of the National University Continuing Education Association.

Effective recruiting and retention strategies for adult literacy programs require systematic efforts.

Recruiting and Retaining Adult Students in Literacy and ABE

Larry G. Martin

Although the resources allocated to and the size and types of providers of adult literacy programs have all increased in recent years, the programs continue to serve fewer than 10 percent of the eligible clients (Development Associates, Inc., 1980). Past attempts to recruit and retain increased numbers of the low-literate population have often obtained mixed results. Some programs enroll a large number and variety of learners and become oversubscribed and overextended as they attempt to address the learning needs of all learners, while other programs in the same communities suffer from low enrollments. One factor contributing to the failure of past efforts to mount consistent and sustained recruiting and retention efforts in particular communities is the absence of knowledge about systematic differences among the low-literate population that might make differential recruitment strategies and program offerings possible (Hayes, 1988). This chapter discusses the twin functions of recruiting and retaining students in adult basic education (ABE) from the perspective of a comprehensive plan for recruiting both students and volunteers.

The marketing approach to recruiting facilitates the systematic efforts of literacy programs to identify and serve specific categories of eligible students and to involve volunteers. Several decision points are particularly important in the development of a comprehensive recruiting plan: identifying categories of subpopulations of potential learners, determining who will be served, determining the needs and interests of those targeted for services, and promoting the program to prospective students and volunteers. These decision points work in concert with the efforts of the program to develop an appropriate product (such as program content, type of diploma or certificate, and so on), place (that is, the location of the program), and price (such as fees, cost of instructional materials, and so on) for a specific type of learner.

Segmenting the Market

Estimates of the number of persons in need of literacy services range from 45 to 70 million. The number of illiterate and functionally illiterate adults who enter this pool each year has been estimated to be about 2.3 million (Fields, Hull, and Sechler, 1987). The primary source of new functional illiterates is those who fail to complete high school (estimated at about 1 million). Other sources include legal and illegal immigrants, refugees, others with limited English proficiency, and those who possess high school diplomas. The percentage of blacks and Hispanics who are functional illiterates is disproportionately high—about 44 percent and 56 percent, respectively.

Market segmentation is a useful metaphor for the process of identifying and categorizing subpopulations of potential learners. It should be possible to reach each segment by a specific mix of the four Ps—product, promotion, place, and price. Three sets of segmentation variables are commonly used: geographic variables (such as distance of learners from the program site), demographic variables (such as age, sex, income, prior education, and occupation), and psychographic variables (such as attitudes, personality, and benefits sought).

There are several advantages to deriving a unified perception of the demographic and psychographic characteristics of individuals who constitute the pool of eligible clients. First, instead of using a shotgun approach, which attempts to serve all eligible learners in a given community, program administrators can identify, target, and monitor the specific subpopulations of learners that their programs are to serve. Second, information about the academic abilities, attitudinal dispositions, environmental constraints, and other characteristics of targeted learners can help administrators to develop comprehensive programs and services that meet learners' specific educational needs. Third, cooperative relationships can be developed and maintained with other literacy providers located in the same geographical areas who target and serve different categories of learners. Fourth, the dropout and attrition rates can be reduced when literacy providers begin to concentrate their limited resources on the students who can benefit most from the specific mix of teachers, volunteers, instructional materials, instructional technology, and classroom environment that their programs can provide.

Typology of Life-Style Differences

The typology of life-style differences among adult high school noncompleters (AHSNCs) presented by Martin (1986) is one approach that practitioners could use to segment the markets served by their programs. The typology was derived from research that used sociodemographic and psychographic characteristics to identify several mutually exclusive categories of AHSNCs. Adult school noncompleters were classified on the basis of their means of financial support and on their degree of socially acceptable behavior. Table 1 shows the results. This section discusses the four primary differentiating characteristics: employment, unemployment, underclass, and age.

The employed group consists of three categories: skilled and unskilled workers (regulars), managers of agencies and organizations (superiors), and owners of businesses (entrepreneurs). These individuals represent a unique target population for adult literacy programs. Functional illiteracy takes a heavy toll on industry as lost productivity, wasted material, damaged machinery, and hazards to employees (Fields, Hull, and Sechler, 1987). As the quality of basic skills preparation becomes increasingly related to productivity and profitability, companies are finding it imperative to become directly involved in the education of their employees.

Table 1. Life-Style Classifications of Adult High School Noncompleters

Means of Financial Support	*Life-Style Classifications*	
	Social	*Antisocial*
Owners of businesses	Entrepreneurs	Underclass entrepreneurs
Managers/supervisors of businesses or agencies	Superiors	Underclass superiors
Skilled/unskilled jobs	Regulars	Underclass regulars
Indirect means of financial support	Suppliants	Underclass suppliants
Recipients of public assistance	Marginals	Underclass marginals

Source: Martin, 1986.

The unemployed group consists of two categories: individuals with an indirect means of financial support (suppliants) and individuals receiving public assistance (marginals). Suppliants tend to be recently unemployed persons receiving unemployment compensation, housewives with minimum labor force experience, Social Security recipients, adults still dependent on their parents, and adults receiving income from other indirect sources. Marginals consist largely of the stationary poor. They are characterized primarily by their lack of economic resources, large families, and single-parent status.

The underclass group is essentially the mirror image of the preceding five categories. Its members share the basic characteristics of each category. However, these individuals are committed to a life-style and a belief system that are antisocial in nature. They are not easily identifiable in the general population, but they can be found in institutions that serve the criminal justice system, such as jails and prisons, and in other rehabilitative social agencies, such as drug detoxication centers and halfway houses. They have a history of drug and alcohol abuse, violence against themselves and others, and crime.

The members of the five social categories can be further distinguished by age into three groups: youthful, young and middle-aged, and older. Youthful noncompleters (ages sixteen to twenty-one) are most likely to have left school recently, and they are often indifferent or hostile toward education, frustrated and embittered by their experiences in school or by chronic unemployment, and lacking self-confidence and encouragement from family and peers. They often are not eager to continue their education, and they are not likely to persist when they do attend (Darkenwald, 1984). Special literacy programs have been developed for youthful noncompleters because they require more structure and prefer learning environments and instructional content that differ from those desired by members of the other age categories (Smith, 1984).

Those in the young and middle-aged adult category (ages twenty-two to fifty-four) enjoy the primary attention of adult literacy programs. However, lack of time is a serious constraint for these adults, especially for those who are more fully engaged in work or family responsibilities (Darkenwald, 1984).

Compared to the members of other age categories, older learners (age fifty-five and older) have the lowest levels of literacy skills and the lowest level of participation in adult literacy programs (Fisher, 1987). One possible cause is incompatibility between their learning needs and the subject matter of adult basic education materials (Fisher, 1987). As programs attempt to address the utilitarian needs of learners to obtain employment and occupational mobility, they often neglect the needs of older learners to adjust to retirement and pursue subject-matter content related to their interests, such as leisure and health.

Targeting the Market

The most successful adult basic education programs target the populations of students whom they seek to serve (Lerche, 1985). Targeting specific learners allows the program to formulate recruitment messages that begin with a clear definition of the program's goals and philosophy and to define objectively the services that it is equipped to provide and the persons whom it is best able to serve. The program's financial, human, and physical resources must enable effective delivery of services. Once a program has clearly delineated its services and stated the intended outcomes of student participation, it can communicate that information to potential students without fear of being unable to deliver on its promises. For example, before a program advertises itself as a GED program for unemployed individuals, such as suppliants and marginals, it should have thought through both the processes and the intended outcomes of the services to be provided.

Researching the Market

In order for a potential learner to relinquish valued resources (such as time with family, potential income, and secure personal perceptions) in order to participate in an adult literacy program, four conditions must be met: The learner must perceive a need for the program, want the program, believe that the program will meet his or her needs and desires, and prefer the provider of the program over all others (Beder, 1986). Knowledge of the learner's needs, wants, beliefs, and preferences is therefore vital to successful recruiting. For example, Hayes and Darkenwald (1988) identified five factors that deterred low-literate adults from participating in adult literacy programs: low self-confidence, social disapproval, situational barriers, negative attitudes to classes, and low personal priority. They found that several factors were statistically associated with demographic characteristics. Their research suggested that situational barriers were positively correlated with being female, unemployed, and having young children. Market research of this nature conducts a carefully designed, systematic analysis of client needs and demand states for particular types of programs.

Kotler (1975) notes three demand states that could explain nonparticipation: negative, none, and latent. In negative demand, the learner actually seeks to avoid the program offered. For example, Quigley (1987) argues that some AHSNCs actively resist enrolling in adult literacy programs for reasons that he terms moral and political indignation. They view the adult literacy program as an extension of the traditional school system that they once rejected. Negative demand is often a problem when there is a solid institutional commitment to a social need that the individual does not perceive as a need. In the case of resisters, the program should critically analyze the expressed needs of these potential learners and offer them viable alternatives.

In the no demand state, potential learners are indifferent to the education offered. Although they do not avoid it, they do not seek it out. This state exists for one of three reasons. First, potential learners may not perceive the value of the program. In this case, the program should connect the offering to some existing need in the marketplace. For example, new computer-based technology is both eliminating unskilled jobs and creating a need for highly knowledgeable and flexible employees. Thus, it increases the demand for industry-based adult literacy programs. Second, there may be little environmental press for the skills that the program offers. If this is suspected, the program should increase its vigilance in the socioeconomic environment to gauge the extent to which the services that it provides are valued in the community. Third, there may be little awareness of the program. In this case, the program should seek to increase its exposure by increasing promotions.

Latent demand exists when there is a genuine need and want for a particular offering, but no offering exists to meet the demand. The response is to develop a new program. For example, in a community in which only adult high school diplomas are available, there may be a latent demand for a more convenient alternative, such as the GED.

The assessment or measurement of learners' needs, wants, beliefs, and preferences can be both formal and informal. Formal assessment is a variant of applied research and must conform to the canons of disciplined inquiry if valid and reliable results are to be obtained (Beder, 1986). Therefore, it is often advisable to confer with a knowledgeable consultant when designing and conducting a formal assessment.

Informal assessment depends on the systematic gathering of data from multiple sources readily accessible to the adult literacy program (Beder, 1986). This type of assessment should be conducted systematically on a continuous basis. When several sources point to a need, a want, a belief, or a perception, the data can be accepted as valid. When the sources conflict, additional confirming or disconfirming information must be sought. Sources of informal needs data include interviews with students, instructors, and employers; analysis of enrollment statistics; feedback at meetings of community groups and professional associations; newspaper articles; research literature; observation in the workplaces or communities of potential learners; and advisory councils.

Promoting Adult Literacy Programs

The function of promotion in adult literacy education is to present accurate and persuasive messages to prospective students, volunteers, donators, and political supporters. Promotional messages can be dramatic or undramatic, simple or complex, shocking or mildly stimulating. Whatever the content or effect, the message should seek on the one hand to stimulate action that overcomes barriers to participation and on the other to present a positive image of the program. For example, promotion by word of mouth may not always be effective, because friends and family who do not approve of educational efforts are not likely to communicate information about adult literacy programs. Therefore, promotional efforts could emphasize the program's individualized, adult-oriented program as a way of combating fears of a competitive environment (Hayes and Darkenwald, 1988). Several approaches have been used successfully to promote adult literacy programs: print media, broadcast media, direct mail, personal contact, telemarketing, and publicity.

Print Media. Print media can be an inexpensive and effective means of communicating the educational services that a program offers to the community at large. However, some potential students are not likely to look at newspapers or even public transport advertisements as sources of information. Information disseminated in print form is most likely to reach students indirectly as a result of word of mouth or referral (Lerche, 1985).

Newspapers are a popular means among adult literacy programs to recruit volunteers. Because most communities are served by newspapers, newspapers are a low-cost and convenient medium for communicating a message to the inhabitants of remote or sparsely populated regions (Falk, 1986). In larger communities where there are many newspapers, individual papers may have different readership profiles. Profiles indicate age, sex, income level, geographic area, and interests of subscribers. Adult literacy programs can use this information to determine which newspaper's readership is closest to the profile of the persons for whom their programs are intended. For example, in many urban communities, students are geographically located in the inner city, while volunteers are located in suburban communities. Volunteers can be recruited via suburban community newspapers, and students can be recruited via inner-city community newspapers. Flexibility is another advantage of newspaper advertising. Advertisements can be large or small. The format can vary greatly: color, copy only, copy and illustrations, and so on. The short lead times for copy submission enable program directors to make last-minute decisions to use newspaper advertisements to increase student enrollments or volunteer participation in programs that have not flourished through other forms of promotion.

Other forms of print media include the vehicles of civic, social, and community organizations (Falk, 1986). These can be magazines, newspapers, or newsletters mailed directly to affinity groups.

Broadcast Media. The broadcast media include both radio and television. These dynamic media provide high impact, permit communication with mass audiences, and have the ability to promote programs for specific geographical areas or selected market segments. Television has the advantage of visual messages. Strong psychological appeals can be made through graphic presentations.

Adult literacy programs operating on modest budgets may not be able to afford the costs of paid broadcast advertising. A thirty-second spot during prime viewing hours on a popular station in a major market will cost several thousand dollars. In addition, because the message may dissipate quickly, it may need to be repeated continuously over an extended period of time. Therefore, the broadcast media are used sparingly in adult literacy education.

Direct Mail. Direct mail advertising offers the advantage of precisely directed messages for well-defined segments of the population (Falk, 1986). Zip codes permit catalogues, pamphlets, bulletins, and descriptive brochures containing a lengthy message to be distributed with precision in geographical marketing segments. Direct-mail advertisements often attempt to encourage recipients to take direct action by clipping and mailing a registration form or a request for more information.

Personal Contact. For many adult literacy programs, personal contact with the people and organizations in their target area is the most effective recruitment technique employed (Lerche, 1985). Formal recruiting calls to persons or organizations thought to be good prospects for the services being promoted allow programs to present a highly personalized, multisensory promotional message and to exercise the tools of persuasion. Personal calls can result in registrations, needed donations, and an ongoing personal relationship with the community. Adult literacy programs use five forms of personal contact: networking, needs assessment surveys, canvassing, public speaking engagements, and word of mouth.

Networking is used to tap the resources and organizations in a community as well as the larger field of adult education professionals. Information about literacy programs can reach potential students via a network of friends, relatives, and neighbors who belong to community organizations or churches with whom the literacy program has made contact as well as through employers and social service agencies (Lerche, 1985). To establish such a network, literacy programs must make conscious efforts to cultivate ties within their community.

One way of working within the community is to set up partnerships with organizations that come into contact with the program's potential student population. Corporations, social service agencies, and secondary schools are typical targets for such partnerships. These organizations can refer students and donate space, equipment, expertise, or support services that the program could not otherwise provide.

Public speaking involves making public presentations at the meetings of local civic groups, charitable organizations, religious organizations, and social clubs. These presentations are reliable ways of providing information, extending the program's network, and raising funds (Lerche, 1985).

Although word of mouth may not be a deliberate recruitment strategy, programmers need to be aware of its effect in the community (Lerche, 1985). The content of other promotional messages and the activities occurring within the program can provide grist for the rumor mill. Therefore, programs should be careful of the image presented in word-of-mouth communications.

Telemarketing. Telemarketing is a proactive and systematic effort to contact current and prospective students and volunteers via telephone and encourage them to participate in the program. It is less expensive than sending representatives into the field to make in-person contacts, yet it is a highly personal way of communicating with prospects and former students. A message can be altered during a conversation as needed, and there is an opportunity for feedback from prospects concerning their perceptions of the program. This technique can be used at any time, and, with proper training from personnel, volunteers and support staff can do the task.

Publicity. Publicity is the nonpaid presentation of information about program activities or personnel by the media. It can be planned or unplanned, and it can present the program in a positive or negative light. Positive publicity about adult literacy program activities or personnel can be used to promote the program or enhance its overall image. Publicity can be a valuable adjunct to paid advertising and other promotional efforts.

The main vehicle used to acquire publicity is the public service announcement (PSA). As a means of featuring information about programs or offerings, adult literacy programs should regularly develop PSAs to document their newsworthy activities. As the result of deregulation, stations are no longer required to run PSAs. Many still do, albeit not in high visibility slots. Therefore, programs seeking publicity should be astute in their relations with the media. Many stations air community bulletin boards that announce special events or new programs. Almost every station conducts a local talk show on which program leaders can volunteer to appear. Finally, program staff members should not hesitate to contact broadcast stations with their ideas for special presentations.

Summary

A comprehensive recruiting plan can significantly enhance a program's ability to serve targeted students effectively. The four decision points presented in this chapter should be viewed as a general framework from which decisions specific to the contextual situation of a given program can be made. Each program must answer four questions: What subpopulations exist in the community? What subpopulations will we serve? How will we identify their specific learning needs? How will we contact potential students and volunteers and interest them in our program?

References

Beder, H. (ed.). *Marketing Continuing Education.* New Directions for Continuing Education, no. 31. San Francisco: Jossey-Bass, 1986.

Darkenwald, G. G. "Continuing Education and the Hard-to-Reach Adult." In G. G. Darkenwald (ed.), *Reaching Hard-to-Reach Adults.* New Directions for Continuing Education, no. 8. San Francisco: Jossey-Bass, 1980.

Darkenwald, G. G. "Participation in Education by Young Adults." In G. G. Darkenwald and A. B. Knox (eds.), *Meeting Educational Needs of Young Adults.* New Directions for Continuing Education, no. 21. San Francisco: Jossey-Bass, 1984.

Development Associates, Inc. *An Assessment of the State-Administered Program of the Adult Education Act: Final Report.* Washington, D.C.: U.S. Department of Education, 1980.

Falk, C. F. "Promoting Continuing Education Programs." In H. Beder (ed.), *Marketing Continuing Education.* New Directions for Continuing Education, no. 31. San Francisco: Jossey-Bass, 1986.

Fields, E. L., Hull, W. L., and Sechler, J. A. *Adult Literacy: Industry-Based Training Programs.* Columbus, Ohio: National Center for Research in Vocational Education, 1987.

Fisher, J. C. "The Literacy Level Among Older Adults: Is It a Problem?" *Adult Literacy and Basic Education,* 1987, *11* (1), 41-50.

Hayes, E. R. "A Typology of Low-Literate Adults Based on Perceptions of Deterrents to Participation in Adult Basic Education." *Adult Education Quarterly,* 1988, *39* (1), 1-10.

Hayes, E. R., and Darkenwald, G. G. "Participation in Basic Education: Deterrents for Low-Literate Adults." *Studies in the Education of Adults,* 1988, *20* (1), 16-28.

Kotler, P. *Marketing for Nonprofit Organizations.* Englewood Cliffs, N.J.: Prentice-Hall, 1975.

Lerche, R. S. *Effective Adult Literacy Programs: A Practitioner's Guide.* New York: Cambridge Books, 1985.

Martin, L. G. "Student's Life-Style Classifications: Key to Improved Literacy Programs." *Lifelong Learning: An Omnibus of Practice and Research,* 1986, *10* (1), 12-15.

Quigley, A. "The Resisters: An Analysis of Nonparticipation in Adult Education." In R. Inkster (ed.), *Proceedings: The Adult Education Research Conference.* Laramie: University of Wyoming, 1987.

Smith, F. B. "High School Equivalency Preparation for Recent Dropouts." In G. G. Darkenwald and A. B. Knox (eds.), *Meeting Educational Needs of Young Adults.* New Directions for Continuing Education, no. 21. San Francisco: Jossey-Bass, 1984.

Larry G. Martin is associate professor of adult and continuing education at the University of Wisconsin–Milwaukee. His research focuses on extending adult education programs to hard-to-reach adults.

The phenomenon of dropout that once plagued correspondence education can be reduced in modern distance education systems by careful recruitment techniques and counseling strategies.

Recruiting and Retaining Adult Students in Distance Education

Michael G. Moore

In distance education, learning and the various activities that we commonly refer to as *studying* and the activities that we refer to as *teaching* occur in different places and usually at different times. The separation of teacher and learner that is the distinguishing characteristic of distance education gives learners certain freedoms that give this form of education its appeal. The kinds of problems that these learners experience are not different from the problems of other learners. However, distance education and traditional forms of education usually draw learners from different populations, and learner problems may affect a larger proportion of distance learners. When problems do occur, they can be exacerbated by distance. For these reasons, retention has always been an issue of special importance in distance education, and it remains a dominant concern.

Retention and recruitment are the responsibilities of one of the three subsystems that make up a modern distance education system. Because the other subsystems are concerned with the production and delivery of programs, they are better known to observers outside the system. The course design subsystem plans and develops course materials, and the communication subsystem delivers these materials through print, broadcasting, recording, or teleconferencing. Recruitment and retention are the work of a third subsystem, which has been called by such names as *student support services, regional services,* and *counseling services.*

Historical Perspective

The oldest form of distance education is correspondence education. Despite the success of broadcasting and other forms of communication, correspondence by mail is still the dominant medium of distance education, not only in less developed countries, as might be expected, but also in North America and in Western Europe. Within such multimedia systems as the British Open University, which gives students a wide range of media options, students consistently invest the majority of their study time in the study of correspondence texts and the preparation of written assignments for their correspondence instructor. Correspondence education provides many of the concepts and provides the basis for many practices of the broader field of distance education, including a long tradition of concern and research into student retention and dropout.

While the history of concern about retention and dropout is probably as old as correspondence education itself, a suitable beginning for our purpose would be the alarm that developed in Madison, Wisconsin, in the late 1950s when the United States Armed Forces Institute, at that time the largest correspondence institution in the world with 300,000 students, discovered that half the students were failing to submit even one assignment and that 90 percent failed to complete their courses (Brittain, 1970).

Following a study of 5,000 students, Bradt (1956) recommended effective counseling at the time of recruitment as well as during the course, especially at the time of the first assignment, as a strategy for reducing the noncompletion rate. James and Wedemeyer (1959) followed up by studying adults taking correspondence courses from the University of Wisconsin. They found that students most likely to drop out of a correspondence course were those who had been uncertain about their goals for taking the course and those who had had difficulty completing the first written assignments. They pointed out the importance of some form of learner support that would help students to clarify their goals at the time of recruitment and to overcome the fears that accompany the submission of their first attempt at writing. A decade of other research efforts followed. These efforts included those of Spencer (1965) at the Pennsylvania State University; Hartsell (1964) at the University of Tennessee; Sloan (1966) at the University of Kentucky; Pfeiffer and Sabers (1970) at the University of Iowa; Donehower (1968) at Nevada; Ball, Kim, and Olmsted (1966) at the University of Washington; and Harter (1969) in New York. The evidence seemed to indicate that the high dropout rate that seemed to be almost inevitable in correspondence education could be decreased or even arrested by a substantial student support effort, especially at the time of recruitment and in the early stages of study.

As with so many aspects of distance education, the event that provided the opportunity for testing and then developing student support as a major component of the distance education system was the establishment in 1969 of the British Open University. Since it began teaching in 1971, the Open University has provided courses for more than a quarter-million adults who had been rejected, failed, overlooked, or unattracted to the conventional educational system. The majority were people whose educational credentials were inadequate for the highly competitive British higher education system. Every year, some 70,000 such persons successfully complete a course at home, studying specially designed tutorials-in-print, which are enriched by television and radio broadcasts, and communicating by mail and telephone with their distant instructors. Another 50,000 adult learners use the same system in a program of noncredit continuing education. Some 200 television programs are made each year, three million study guides are dispatched, and almost a million correspondence assignments are marked and commented on. This system has become the standard and the model of contemporary distance education. It has been emulated throughout the world. It has its analogues in the U.S.A. Similar universities have been set up in Spain, Israel, West Germany, Canada, Pakistan, Venezuela, Costa Rica, Thailand, the Netherlands, Sri Lanka, Hong Kong, Japan, Italy, Indonesia, and India (Rumble and Harry, 1982).

Opinion at the Open University is almost unanimous in attributing its success to two factors above all others. Good distance education, it is believed, depends on high-quality course design and on equally high-quality student support. Perhaps the best evidence of the importance given to the student support subsystem is provided by an examination of the University's accounts showing that, compared with the more than £25 million (roughly $37 million) spent in 1986 on faculty and academic support, slightly more was spent on the student support functions of what are called the Regional Academic Services.

The number of adults in the U.S.A. who currently pursue university education through distance teaching is four times as large as the number in Great Britain. In contrast to Great Britain's national delivery system, America's is pluralistic, shared as it is by the independent study divisions of more than seventy universities. In addition to the universities, private institutions that are members of the National Home Study Council provide courses, mostly of a vocational nature, to some four million persons (Ludlow, 1987). The armed forces deliver their own programs, with as many as 400,000 involved in the distance education program of the Air Force alone (Savarico, 1987). Some 200 Fortune 500 corporations use distance education in their in-house training programs. More than 600,000 people have taken courses provided by the Adult Learning Service of the Public Broadcasting Service (Brock, 1987). To the large numbers being served by these well-established media we should add the unknown but almost certainly very large population involved in programs through audio, video, and computer telecommunications media. Among the best-known of the projects in this area are the Electronic University, the National Technological University, and the National University Teleconference Network, the last two linking member universities in a satellite-borne communications system that delivers educational resources beyond the capacity of the individual institutions.

An especially noteworthy feature of recent distance education at the university level has been the stimulation of the development of high-quality multi-media programs for large-scale national use by the Annenberg/CPB Project. Designed by course teams with million-dollar budgets, such courses as "The Mechanical Universe," "The Africans," "Planet Earth," and "The Constitution" have most of the characteristics of courses designed and delivered by Open Universities in other countries. What we are witnessing in the U.S.A. in the absence of the establishment of an integrated national distance education system (a decision that has been made in other countries by a central policy-making organ) is the growth of various cells of such a system, or perhaps of parallel systems, through a process of voluntary networking and consortium building. The evolving systems are assuming most of the features of the more formally established distance education systems overseas. However, the student support subsystem is considerably less well developed in American distance education than the communication and course design subsystems. It is vital for the American systems to appreciate the significance of learner support, and it is necessary to look at foreign systems to understand why.

Functions of the Learner Support System

Distance education systems have either been established by governments to fill a gap in the public provision of education or by universities or private organizations to fill perceived gaps in the conventional system. By its very nature, access to distance education is more open than access to conventional education. Seventy percent of the university-level correspondence programs in the United States and Canada have no educational prerequisites for admission (Feasley, 1983). Courses offered in the private sector are open to all. The Open University provides heavily subsidized courses (some 80 percent of tuition being paid to government) on a first-come, first-served basis. Admission is open to all, regardless of previous education experience. Athabasca University in Canada and Everyman's University in Israel have equally open admissions policies.

Given the expectations of those who fund and organize distance education that it will open opportunity to those to whom it would otherwise be denied, recruitment becomes a matter of particular importance. The communication resources already employed for instruction are applied to the task of informing potential learners of the availability of opportunity. Newspaper advertisements, radio and television announcements, news releases, and direct mailings lead the recruitment techniques. Meetings can be organized for interested persons, whose questions can be answered by institutional representatives. Advisory services that can be contacted by telephone can be established.

These and other techniques have been so successful at the British Open University that there are more twice as many applicants—some 45,000—for admission each year as teaching resources can accommodate. Surveys have been taken over a number of years of the impact of the various publicity techniques. Better-educated, middle-class adults are more aware of Open University opportunities than poorly educated working-class people. They apply sooner, and they are less diffident about seeking advice, with the result that the already fairly well-educated enjoy this continuing education opportunity to a disproportionate extent. Given the higher tuition costs in American distance education, a similar phenomenon almost certainly exists here also.

The most extensive study of student dropout in recent years has been that of Woodley and Parlett (1983). While allowances must be made for differences in the ways in which institutions measure retention, Woodley and Parlett were able to reach the following conclusions: The average wastage rate for courses at Canada's Athabasca University was 71 percent. However, the proportion dropped to 42 percent if the base was taken to be those students who submitted the first assignment. In Canada's Open Learning Institute, 32 percent of the students who submitted a first assignment dropped out (p. 3). In the U.S.A., a study by the National University Continuing Education Association of member institution courses reached the conclusion that six of every ten who enrolled completed their courses; more than seven in ten of those who submitted at least one assignment went on to complete all written work (p. 3). At the N.K.I. School in Norway, which offers technical and vocational programs, between 65 percent and 80 percent of enrollees completed at least one course (p. 4). At West Germany's Fernuniversität, 47 percent of the students who completed one year's study did not register for a course in the subsequent year (p. 4). At the British Open University, 71 percent of the students who registered completed their year's course (p. 3). While it is difficult to generalize from these findings, it appears that about 70 percent of the students who commit themselves to the extent of completing one assignment are likely to complete their course.

Why Do Students Drop Out?

When students are asked to report their study difficulties, planning and scheduling problems appear high on their lists. In a study of some 1,000 students, Murgatroyd (1982) found that more than half had experienced difficulties with planning and organizing their time. Also high on their lists of student problems was the tension between the demands of part-time study and those posed by family and friends: "My husband just cannot see the point of my studying. He says he doesn't know why I bother. Whilst this doesn't stop me from doing it, it doesn't really give me the right framework to perform at my best, does it?" (Murgatroyd, 1982, p. 84). In this study, about one student in four expressed reservations of the kind just noted. A third source of discouragement derives from the unrealistic expectations with which learners often undertake distance education. No fewer than 45 percent of the students in Murgatroyd's (1982) sample stated that they were looking for promotion at work or change of job. Some of the intended changes, such as from farming or mining to teaching or administration and management, were very substantial, and disappointment and perhaps dropout seemed a likely result. Finally, while students do not report anxiety as a problem, it does appear to be an underlying factor in many of the other problems to which they attach importance. Murgatroyd (1982) evaluated both general levels of anxiety and specific anxieties. The data showed that 23 percent of the students had a high (+1 standard deviation) specific-anxiety score—that is, high anxiety about such specific aspects of study as examinations, the ability to remember, and getting good grades. However, specific anxiety was only slightly related to academic performance. It would seem that students who drop out of courses because of anxiety about such matters as examinations could be counseled against unrealistic concerns, while those who perform badly might need help with a perhaps unrecognized, unnecessary, yet damaging general level of anxiety.

Woodley and Parlett (1983) attribute dropout to a range of factors: course factors, study environment factors, motivational factors, and other factors. Students are more likely to abandon a course that is badly designed, or that has a work load far in excess of its credit rating, or that is unsatisfactory in content than they are to drop a good course. Many variables can disappoint, including unhelpful correspondence instructors, difficulty in receiving broadcast programs, and slow response to inquiries. Study environment factors often cited as problems include illness of student or relative, change in marital status, having a baby, and moving. Work-related problems include increased work hours or responsibilities, being sent abroad, or changing jobs. Changes in financial circumstances and lack of encouragement by spouse or employer are other important factors. As far as motivational factors are concerned, students withdraw when they have achieved the goals that led them to study. This can mean not completing the course. Similarly, they withdraw if their goals change or if a better way of achieving them presents itself. The other factors cited by Woodley and Parlett (1983) include fear of examinations and "accidents," such as turning up for the wrong examinations or for the wrong course.

Nicholson (1977) adds four others to the learner problems just listed. First, for many distance learners there is a deficit of skills. In almost all sectors of higher education today, there are some students who may be educationally disadvantaged because they lack basic skills in reading, note taking, essay writing, test taking, and time management, but these are especially serious handicaps for the adult distance learner. Second, problems arise from role conflicts, which include conflicts between student and family roles and between student and work roles. Nicholson (1977) believes that emotional adjustment to distance learning, where students work in isolation and are therefore denied the comfort of being in a learner community, can also pose problems. Finally, he suggests that problems can arise from changes in the personality or life-style that often accompany learning. To experience a new way of life within the setting of one's old life, he suggests, can impose unmanageable strains on familial and occupational relations. Further, although the student may eagerly embrace any changes that take place in his or her cognitive structure, the changes may not be consonant with more ingrained beliefs and habits. The overall cumulative effect on the person can be, at least initially, disintegrative.

The Systems' Response: Supporting the Learner

In distance education, the recruitment and the retention of learners are the work of the student support services. These services can consist of no more than a toll-free number giving access to one or two full-time counselors in the Independent Study Division of the university or of a multimillion-dollar subsystem employing hundreds of counselors, as at the Open University. In some cases, instructors are expected to handle student problems along with their teaching work. In others, they can refer to specialist helpers. They may be expected to respond on the basis of common sense and general knowledge, or they may receive special training in this work.

The most sophisticated system is that of the Open University of the United Kingdom, which has become a model of effective student support. The basic aim of student support services of the Open University is to offset the impersonality of centrally produced course materials and the mass media used in communication by providing the student with an adviser who is accessible, preferably locally, who has knowledge of the individual student, and who is qualified to help the student. At the Open University, each new student is provided with the name of a part-time counselor upon admission and before beginning study. Counselors have many years' experience of the demands and problems of distance education. Their caseloads number about fifty. Counselors are located nationwide, and most are within easy travel distance of their students. The counselor writes to the new student explaining his or her availability and inviting the student to a preliminary meeting. Throughout the following year of study, the counselor receives regular reports on the student's progress and intervenes on his or her initiative as well as in response to requests from the learner for help. Each student and each counselor is allocated to a study center—a site in the vicinity, usually a school or college, where meeting facilities are available. Counselors are provided with expenses to travel and can arrange to meet students as needed at the study center. They receive extra stipends when emergency meetings are necessary, and they are paid to attend in-service training sessions to ensure their continued understanding of both the university system and of counseling theory and practice in general. As well as responding to crises, counselors organize special sessions to deal with such issues as selecting future courses, deciding about career change, learning about funding resources, and developing study skills and examination techniques. Similar but not identical counseling systems have been established in the open universities of Spain, Venezuela, and Athabasca, while almost every one of the more than twenty national distance teaching universities throughout the world has adopted the use of study centers (Rumble and Harry, 1982). In the U.S.A., perhaps the closest replication of the decentralized counseling model was the University of Wisconsin Community Based Educational Counseling Service, a statewide system that maintained some twenty-three counselors in different parts of the state at such locations as public libraries, courthouses, and extension offices (Thompson and Jensen, 1977).

There are a variety of other models for student support services. One has been mentioned: A professional counselor is located at the educational institution, and students access the counselor either by travelling to the institution or by letter and telephone. Since high-quality distance education depends on the economies of scale that are obtained by producing materials for large numbers of students, it is difficult to see how there could be enough full-time counselors to have personal knowledge of more than a small proportion of the student body. Another model of counseling uses itinerant counselors; this approach can be found in Australia (Coltman, 1983) and in Canada (Salter, 1982), where the North Island College provides a mobile study center in a mobile motor home. However, the close rapport that seems to be the basis for a good counseling relationship can hardly be established in this way, and it does not seem desirable for students to have to postpone the management of their concerns until the counselor next passes through the locality.

Conclusion

A great deal is known about the problems and needs of adult learners in distance education. The numbers of adults engaged in this form of education run into the millions, and as the newer open universities develop their research programs we can hope to learn even more about the learner in such settings. Much is known about ways of supporting the distant learner and thus of retaining the distant learner within the learning system. Although more needs to be known here, too, it appears that what is required in this regard in the U.S.A. is not so much more information as it is the political will within educational organizations to invest the money and personnel that good learner support requires. The work of the Annenberg/CPB Project is helping universities and colleges to discover the benefits of collaborating in course design and development, and the telecommunications consortia are showing the benefits of cooperating for large-scale program delivery. We can look forward to a future when these initiatives will result in the rationalization of program design and delivery resources. Then we will look for a reorganization of the resources that will be needed to provide every would-be distant learner with the necessary admissions advice and continuing counseling throughout the learning career. The elements of such a system exist in colleges and universities, private schools, the corporate and public training sector, public libraries, and the telecommunications networks. At the present time, too many educators are employed in the roles of content delivery in classrooms, a highly inefficient form of craft teaching, and too few are available for the more critical activities of counseling and giving support to distance learners. A fundamental paradigm shift in education is now called for.

References

Ball, S. J., Kim, H. Y., and Olmsted, A. D. *Correspondence Study Evaluation Project, Stage 1.* Seattle: University of Washington, 1966. (ED 010 862)

Bradt, K. H. "Servicemen Who Take Correspondence Courses: A Research Report of Their Problems." *Journal of Educational Research*, 1956, *50*, 113-119.

Brittain, C. *Strategies for Improving Correspondence Courses and the Role of Educational Research.* Madison, Wis.: United States Armed Forces Institute, 1970.

Brock, D. "And Six to Grow On." *American Journal of Distance Education*, 1987, *1* (2), 34-43.

Coltman, B. "Environment and Systems in Distance Counseling." In *International Workshop on Counseling in Distance Education Selected Papers.* Cambridge, England: Open University, 1983.

Donehower, G. M. *Variables Associated with Correspondence Students: A Study to Test Twelve Hypotheses.* Reno: Correspondence Division, University of Nevada, 1968. (ED 016 925)

Feasley, C. *Serving Learners at a Distance: A Guide to Program Practices.* Washington, D.C.: Association for the Study of Higher Education, 1983.

Harter, D. *Why SUNY Students Fail to Complete Independent Study Courses.* Albany: State University of New York, 1969. (ED 035 814)

Hartsell, C. "Correspondence Dropouts: Why?" *Adult Leadership,* 1964, *13,* 156.

James, B. J., and Wedemeyer, C. "Completion of University Correspondence Courses by Adults." *Home Study Review,* 1959, *30,* 87-93.

Ludlow, N. "Interview with M. Lambert." *American Journal of Distance Education,* 1987, *1* (2), 67-71.

Murgatroyd, S. "Student Learning Difficulties and the Role of Regional Support Services." *Institutional Research Review,* 1982, *1,* 81-100.

Nicholson, N. "Counseling the Adult Learner in the Open University." *Teaching at a Distance,* 1977, *8,* 62-69.

Pfeiffer, J. W., and Sabers, D. *Attrition and Achievement in Correspondence Study.* Washington, D.C.: National Home Study Council, 1970. (ED 036 707)

Rumble, G., and Harry, K. (eds.). *The Distance Teaching Universities.* London: Croom-Helm, 1982.

Salter, D. "Mobile Learning Centers in an Open Learning System." In J. Daniel, A. Stroud, and J. Thompson (eds.), *Learning at a Distance: A World Perspective.* Edmonton, Alberta: Athabasca University, 1982.

Savarise, P. "Interview with W. Wojciechowski." *American Journal of Distance Education,* 1987, *1* (3), 67-71.

Sloan, D. "Survey Study of University Dropouts and Cancellations." *Home Study Review,* 1966, *7,* 9-16.

Spencer, O. "Factors Associated with Persons Who Complete Correspondence Courses." *Home Study Review,* 1965, *5,* 10-24.

Thompson, C., and Jensen, D. *Community-Based Educational Counseling for Adults.* Madison: University of Wisconsin, 1977.

Woodley, A., and Parlett, M. "Student Dropout." *Teaching at a Distance,* 1983, *24,* 2-23.

Michael G. Moore is associate professor of adult education at Pennsylvania State University, director of the American Center for the Study of Distance Education, and editor of the American Journal of Distance Education.

Tying training programs directly to a corporation's management systems, such as strategic planning and succession planning, minimizes the need for human resources professionals to focus on recruitment and retention.

Recruiting and Retaining Adult Students in HRD

Diane Roemer Yarosz

One of the criteria for successful companies outlined by Peters and Waterman (1983) is staying close to the customer. Staying close to the customer requires attention from human resources professionals, who include planners, course developers, and trainers. Typically, we think of the customer as the consumer who pays so many dollars for such and such a product or service. Many human resources professionals in business and industry view their internal customer in the same way. Both the business organization and its employees are customers. Both are consumers of products or services developed by human resources planners, course developers, and trainers. Business and industry spent an estimated $32 billion on formal training in 1987; $22.4 billion was budgeted for the payroll of the human resources professionals who planned, designed, developed, produced, and delivered the training programs (Geber, 1987). Employees invested 1,195.8 million hours in training in 1987 (Geber, 1987). To maintain the level of expenditure on training, human resources professionals have found effective ways of staying close to their customers and of ensuring that the right training is delivered to the right customer. This chapter views the organization and its employees as customers of human resources planners, course developers, and trainers. Two topics are emphasized: needs identification and recruitment.

P. S. Cookson (ed.). *Recruiting and Retaining Adult Students.*
New Directions for Continuing Education, no. 41. San Francisco: Jossey-Bass, Spring 1989. 99

Needs Identification

Human resources planners, course developers, and trainers spend a great deal of time conducting needs analysis surveys to identify training and development opportunities. These surveys poll employees regarding perceived needs that in the employees' view require attention. These perceived needs can reflect interests in general management and employee development topics, such as planning, organizing, and decision making, or in specific functional topics, such as finance, marketing, and manufacturing. The customers—the organization's employees—may base their needs assessment on current training activities that the organization already offers or as a reaction to external hot topics. For example, when quality circles were popular, many employees wanted courses in quality circle techniques, even in organizations that were not ready to adopt quality circles. The risk in using needs analysis surveys is that the employees' perceived training needs may not be the organization's needs.

To minimize the risk of assessing perceived needs rather than real needs, human resources professionals are forming close alliances with their customers, the organization and its employees, and using four management systems or processes to identify training and development needs: strategic planning, succession planning, the performance management system, and the career management system.

Strategic Planning. The first process that human resources professionals use to identify training and development needs is strategic planning. Many corporations devote several months each year to the strategic planning process. The process enables business units to plan where they should direct their efforts over the next three, five, and ten years. Often, human resources and training groups play a key role in the planning process by focusing on the human resources needs of the business. For example, a company may decide to increase the number of products that it will develop, produce, and market over the next five years. Proactively, it will need to increase its employees in research and development, manufacturing, marketing, sales, and support functions. A substantial increase in employees may require expansion of the human resources and training functions. New employees will need to be recruited, oriented to corporate structure and values, and trained in general management and employee skills and in the functional skills required for their specific jobs. The corporation as customer may decide to expand into new markets. The training function might respond by retraining the marketing and sales departments on ways of dealing with the new market and the company's new competitors. As a result of strategic planning, the human resources and training functions identify the future training needs of its customer the corporation.

Succession Planning. Succession planning is the second process that human resources professionals use to identify training and development needs. After the corporation has completed its strategic planning process and mapped its future directions, human resources planners assist the corporation in identifying key positions needed to implement the plans and in profiling the critical qualifications and skills that the holders of key positions must have. After the key positions have been profiled, incumbents (employees holding the positions) and their managers identify successors (or replacements) for them. The critical qualifications and skills of the key positions are matched with the qualifications and skills of successors in order to determine training and development needs. For example, a corporation that is already marketing its products to European countries may want to expand its markets to Japan and the Mideast within the next two years. The profile of the key position responsible for this market expansion would need to include skills in global marketing. The incumbent who has been responsible for European marketing might need development in such topics as global marketing, competitive analysis, and cultural differences. Then the profiles of potential successors are matched with the key position profiles to determine development needs. Before the potential successor moves into the position, he or she must be trained in global marketing, competitive analysis, and cultural differences. The succession planning process identifies the current and future training needs of incumbents and successors to the key positions required for the implementation of strategic plans.

Performance Management System. The strategic planning process provides input into the performance management system. The performance management system follows the business objectives set forth in the strategic plan down through the organization. The system involves planning, developing, and appraising employee performance. Training needs are identified during each phase of the system.

Planning. Performance planning begins at the end of each business year and is completed during the first quarter of the following year. Highlight reports written by employees provide monthly feedback to managers on the achievement of results, but reports are not the only method through which employees communicate with managers. Feedback discussions held on an ongoing basis inform managers of how employees are progressing and of any changes in objectives. Performance planning identifies what is expected of each member of an organization and how he or she will be measured in achieving those objectives.

Development. After the manager and the employee plan the employee's performance, they identify the core job skills required for achievement of the objectives. Managers and employees can identify the skills that are important in achieving objectives. In this way, managers can develop employees proactively. That is, the employees can concentrate on developing the skills needed to accomplish objectives. The development plan can be followed up by human resources staff, who identify training programs aimed at developing the necessary skills.

Throughout the year, development discussions between the manager and the employee maintain an ongoing dialogue regarding the implementation of performance and skill development plans. When performance is positive, the development discussion can focus on development opportunities that will enhance the employee's responsibilities and skills. When performance needs improvement, the manager helps the employee to analyze the situation, solve the problem, and plan specific actions and deadlines.

Appraisal. Since the manager and the employee have agreed on the objectives to be accomplished at the beginning of the year and since they have been involved in development discussions throughout the year, the employee is not surprised when his or her accomplishments and skills are formally appraised. The appraisal discussion is a review of the past that enables the manager and the employee to discuss how well objectives were accomplished and how the skills needed to perform the job were demonstrated. Such a review is a two-way problem-solving discussion, not a report card. The review becomes the logical third step in the performance management system. This review of the past feeds back to the first step in the system in that employee and manager develop an improvement plan with action steps and target dates. The improvement plan can be followed up by human resources staff, who recommend training and development programs to assist in the overall development plan.

Organizations have found that appraisal systems are effective if they allow for frequent communication between manager and employee, specify job expectations, provide for accurate evaluations, and solve problems. Top performance results from a performance management system directed tied to the corporation's strategic and business plans. The system links every employee to these plans and helps to demonstrate how the contributions and accomplishments of each employee help the employee to develop professionally and personally. By identifying current training needs, the performance management system assists employees in accomplishing their objectives and thus enables the corporation to accomplish its strategic plans.

Career Management System. An integral part of both the succession planning and the performance management system, the career management system is another process that human resources professionals use to identify training and development needs. Through the career management system, employees make the corporation aware of their personal goals, aspirations, and development and training needs. There are three elements in the career management system: assessment, planning, and development.

Assessment. In the assessment phase, employees assess their career interests, values, and personality characteristics and compare their career options with their self-assessments. They determine whether they want to change jobs, what jobs are available, and job requirements, and they compare their interests, knowledge, and skills with what a new job requires.

Planning. In the planning phase, employees develop a specific plan for achieving their career goal by identifying their career decision or goal, when they want to achieve it, how they can achieve it, and what resources are needed to achieve it.

Development. During the development phase, employees implement their plans by determining how they can improve in their present position before assuming a new position. The performance management system is used to identify current performance development and training needs.

The career management system identifies the current and future training needs of employees who are interested in moving forward. This career information is fed into the succession planning process, forming a match between the organization's succession plans and the career plans of employees.

All four management systems enable human resources planners, course developers, and trainers to identify training needs that are based on corporate and individual objectives. By linking the accomplishment of objectives to the real need for training, human resources professionals minimize the number of employees who attend programs because they "think" they need to learn a particular skill, even if it is not necessary for their job.

Recruitment

The preceding section discussed four management systems that assist human resources professionals in helping managers and employees to identify employee training needs. These systems minimize the need for recruitment by trainers, since enrollment in training is part of the process. However, there are three situations in which employees are recruited into training programs: selection by management, self-selection, and job status change.

Selection by Management. Course developers and trainers design and deliver training programs with goals that range from developing general management skills for top-level management to developing premanagement skills for potential new managers. The need for these programs arises from the strategic and succession planning processes. For example, if a corporation determines that its upper-level management lacks such critical skills as strategic leadership and planning, course developers or external consultants design a program aimed at developing these skills. Instead of sending all upper-level managers to the program, top-level management nominates candidates for the program. A selection committee reviews the recommendations of top management and identifies program participants. These names are then forwarded to the training department.

Self-Selection. When the training department distributes a flyer on a new internal or external training program, employees may obtain approval from their manager to attend the program. The program may be one that was not available when the manager and the employee discussed the development plan that is tied to the employee's objectives as part of the performance management system. Some corporations make tuition aid available to employees that enables employees who have the approval of their manager to enroll in a degree-granting program.

When employees enroll in degree-granting programs that are directly linked to career objectives, they are more likely to receive recognition for their efforts than they are in the absence of such linkage. The key to self-selection is tying the training and development program to performance and career objectives that the manager and the employee have discussed and agreed on.

Job Status Change. Managers enroll employees in training programs who are new in the company or who have assumed a new job or new responsibilities. For example, most corporations require new sales representatives to attend between two and twenty weeks of training before they are allowed to sell.

Summary

Human resources professionals use such management systems as strategic planning, succession planning, the performance management system, and the career management system to identify the training needs of the organization and its employees. Tying training programs directly to these management systems minimizes the need for human resources professionals to focus on recruitment and retention. The organization and its employees are aware of the skills that they need in order to accomplish their strategic, individual performance, and career objectives. When the need for training is not obvious or when a traditional needs assessment survey is used to identify it, it is more difficult for human resources planners, course developers, and trainers to recruit trainees. Thus, when training becomes an integral part of the process in achieving objectives, training is more important, and human resources professionals are viewed as major contributors to the success of the corporation and its employees.

References

Geber, B. "Training Budgets Still Healthy." *Training*, 1987, *24*, 39-45.
Peters, T., and Waterman, R. *In Search of Excellence.* New York: Warner Books, 1983.

Diane Roemer Yarosz is the director of human resources planning and development at E. R. Squibb and Sons, Inc., Princeton, New Jersey.

This chapter summarizes the effective recruitment and retention practices presented in preceding chapters.

Recruiting and Retaining Adult Students: Guidelines for Practice

Peter S. Cookson

The preceding chapters review multiple strategies for a multiplicity of continuing education settings whereby adult and continuing education practitioners can enhance the capacity of their respective organizations to recruit and retain adult students. Recruitment was defined in Chapter One as those steps in the program planning process taken to induce prospective adult students to participate in programs of sponsored learning. Retention was defined as the capacity of the continuing education program to transform initial commitment into continuing participation.

This chapter summarizes the conclusions of preceding chapters that transcend particular settings. Building on the practice framework presented in Chapter One, the guidelines presented in the next two sections incorporate the salient elements highlighted by chapter authors.

The two organizational theories described in Chapter Two provide insights into the possible reasons for their salience. Compliance theory emphasizes the nature of the relationship between continuing education practitioners, the program, and the organizational sponsor on the one hand and program participants on the other. It suggests that, wherever possible, continuing education programs should accentuate normative over either remunerative or coercive relationships. Open-systems theory emphasizes the need for harmony and complementarity among a system's subsystems. Harmony and complementarity increase the likelihood that program goals, faculty and staff, organizational structure, psychological climate, and leadership are all oriented toward accommodating the learning needs and interests of prospective and actual adult students.

Guidelines for Recruitment

• Conduct effective public relations to inform and favorably impress relevant publics—prospective adult students, their important others, and other organizations with which collaborative relationships may be formed—with respect to the organizational sponsor and the range of programs that it offers.
• Develop sound, differentiated marketing strategies that include mapping the designated population of actual markets, potential markets, and nonmarkets; identifying specific and multiple market segments; and assessing the learning needs, intentions, beliefs, and attitudes of prospective adult students and their important others.
• Promote the program by advertising program availability and both the instrumental and the expressive benefits of participation via all communication channels appropriate to the target categories of prospective adult students.
• Guide learners into learning activities. Use preenrollment information and orientation sessions, appropriate admissions and registration procedures, and access to counseling and advising to communicate the correspondence between students' learning objectives and the program's objectives.

Guidelines for Retention

• Ensure high-quality educational programming.
• Continue a range of high-quality and accessible student support services, including advising and counseling, hassle-free registration and admissions procedures, financial assistance, encouragement of peer support groups, and continuing interpretation of learning activities to adult students' important others.
• Offer high-quality instruction that provides effective and personable learning experiences and positive group experiences.
• Engage adult students in program governance. Establish and use structures for mutual planning. Demonstrate that the program is responsive to formative, summative, and impact evaluations of and by adult students.
• Establish program continuity by linking the program to prerequisite and succeeding programs. Package the program so as to promote the

formation of long-term institutional loyalty to the sponsor and its other programs. Establish rituals and symbols that help to form a sense of shared meaning and connectedness among students, their important others, and program faculty and staff.

Peter S. Cookson is associate professor of adult education and professor in charge of the Adult Education Program at Pennsylvania State University.

Index

A

Aasheim, L. J., 51, 52, 61
Abler, W., 7, 11
Academic advising, for adult students, 58
Academic Self-Concept Scale (ASCS-R), 54
Achtziger, M. A., 52, 61
Adaptive strategy, for recruitment, 67-69
Admissions: for adult students, 53-55; open, 92-93
Adult basic education (ABE). *See* Literacy and adult basic education
Adult students: academic success and persistence factors for, 55-56; admissions for, 53-55, 92-93; approaches to higher education by, 49-62; aspects of recruiting and retaining, 3-11; attrition of, 56-57, 94-95; background on, 49; community of, 74-76; in continuing higher education, 63-78; in continuing professional education, 35-48; in distance education, 89-98; guidelines for practice with, 107-109; and human resources development, 99-105; institutional responses to, 57-59, 95-97; literacy programs for, 79-88; marketing to, 23-33; and organizational theory, 13-22; participation trends by, 50-51; recruiting, 51-53; summary on, 59-60; support services for, 90-98
Ajzen, I., 37, 47, 48
Alienative involvement, 14, 15
American College Testing Program, 30, 32
Andersen, C. J., 53-54, 60
Anderson, P. E., 10, 17
Annenberg/CPB Project, 92, 97
Appraisal, in human resources development, 102. *See also* Assessment; Evaluation
Apps, J., 50-51, 60
Aslanian, C. B., 51, 60

Assessment: in human resources development, 103; and literacy market research, 84. *See also* Appraisal; Evaluation; Needs assessment
Athabasca University (Canada), and distance education, 92, 93, 96
Attitude: formation and change of, 42-44; in participation model, 37-40
Attrition, reasons for, 56-57, 94-95. *See also* Retention
Australia, distance education counseling in, 96

B

Ball, S. J., 90, 97
Bangladesh, remunerative power in, 15
Bean, J. P., 56, 57, 59, 60, 72, 74, 77
Beaudin, B., 8, 10
Beder, H., 24, 27, 32, 69, 70, 77, 83, 84, 88
Behavior, in participation model, 38-39
Beliefs, in participation model, 39-41
Bezold, C., 44, 47
Bidwell, C. E., 8, 10
Bishop, J., 51, 60
Bitterman, J., 58, 60
Boshier, R. W., 6, 7, 10, 36, 47
Bradt, K. H., 90, 97
Brickwell, H. M., 51, 60
Brittain, C., 90, 97
Broadcast media, for literacy promotion, 85-86
Brock, D., 92, 97
Brockett, R. G., 2
Buckmaster, A., 26, 32

C

C. W. Post Center, Brentwood campus, Women's Project at, 52
Cagiano, A., 55, 60
Calculative involvement, 14, 15, 21

111

California at Berkeley, University of, and continuing professional education, 26
Campbell, J. F., 53, 60, 70, 71, 73, 77
Canada, distance education in, 91, 92, 93, 96
Career management system, in human resources development, 102-103
Carlson, R., 44, 47
Carp, A., 13, 16, 22
Caulley, D. N., 40, 48
Chaffee, E. E., 67, 69-70, 77
Clarke, J. H., 59, 60
Coercive power, 14, 15, 21
College Board, 54
College-Level Examination Program (CLEP), 54
Collins, J. B., 36, 47
Collins, M., 74, 77
Coltman, B., 96, 97
Comadena, M. E., 55, 60
Communication, channels of, for promotion, 7
Community of learners, in continuing higher education, 74-76
Competitive strategies, for recruitment, 68
Compliance theory, of organizations, 14-16
Continuing education: in distance education, 89-98; guidelines for, 107-109; in higher education, 49-62; and human resources development, 99-105; in literacy and adult basic education, 79-88; marketing for, 23-33; and organizational theory, 13-22; practices in, 3-11
Continuing higher education (CHE): adult students in, 63-78; concept of, 63; longitudinal and cross-sectional perspectives for, 73; packaging in, 71-72; participation in, 64; program and participation interface in, 65-67; recruitment in, 67-72; retention in, 72-76; summary on, 76. *See also* Higher education
Continuing professional education (CPE): aspects of participation in, 35-48; and government control, 26-27; increasing and enhancing participation in, 41-47; participation model for, 37-41

Cookson, P. S., 1-22, 36, 47, 107-109
Coombs, F. S., 37, 48
Cooperative strategies, for recruitment, 68-69
Coordination, in organizations, 18
Correspondence education. *See* Distance education
Costa Rica, open university in, 91
Cotten, C. C., 53, 60
Coupling, loose and tight, 66, 71
Courtney, B. C., 47, 48
Cross, K. P., 36, 47

D

Darkenwald, G. G., 2, 4, 10, 36, 40, 46, 47, 48, 68, 70, 77, 82, 83, 85, 88
Davidson, A. R., 37, 48
de la Croix de la Fayette, J-M., 57, 60
Demand categories, and marketing, 25-26
Demand states, and literacy program participation, 83-84
Development, in human resources development, 101-102, 103
Development Associates, 79, 88
DeWees, P., 52, 59, 61
Differentiation, in organization, 18
Direct mail, for literacy promotion, 86
Distance education: aspects of, 89-98; background on, 89-90; conclusion on, 97; dropout reasons in, 94-95; extent of, 91-92; history of, 90-92; retention efforts by, 95-97; student support system in, 92-93
Donaldson, J. F., 2, 63-78
Donehower, G. M., 90, 98
Dropouts, reasons of, 56-57, 94-95

E

Electronic University, and distance education, 92
Emery, F. E., 65, 77
Empire State College, orientation by, 58
Energy, importation of, in organizations, 16-17
Entropy, negative, in organizations, 17
Equifinality, in organizations, 18
Escott, M. D., 55, 60

113

Ethical issues, in marketing and planning, 24
Etzioni, A., 14-16, 22
Evaluation, formative and summative, for enhancing participation, 46-47. See also Appraisal; Assessment
Everyman's University (Israel), open admission to, 92
Exchange, and recruitment, 68

F

Falk, C. F., 24, 26, 32, 85, 86, 88
Feasley, C., 92, 98
Fernuniversitat (West Germany), retention at, 93
Fidler, D. S., 58, 60
Fields, E. L., 80, 81, 88
Fishbein, M., 37, 40, 47, 48
Fisher, J. C., 82, 88
Frederick, D., 55, 61
Freedman, L., 64, 77

G

Gallien, K. J., 52, 53, 60
Geber, B., 99, 105
Geisler, M., 55, 60
General Educational Development (GED), 54, 83, 84
Germany, Federal Republic of, open university in, 91, 93
Glen Ellen, Illinois, marketing research in, 30
Goals and values subsystem, of organizations, 19
Goodnow, B., 30, 32
Governance factors, and retention, 9
Government control, and continuing professional education, 26-27
Griffith, W. S., 1, 23-33
Grotelueschen, A. D., 40, 48
Group experience: in continuing higher education, 74-76; and marketing, 28-29; and retention, 8-9; for support, 59

H

Harry, K., 91, 96, 98
Harter, D., 90, 98
Hartsell, C., 90, 98
Hayes, E. R., 79, 83, 85, 88

Hentschel, D., 70, 71, 73, 77
Hexter, H., 53-54, 60
Hickson, D. J., 14, 22
Higher education: academic success and persistence in, 55-56; admissions to, 53-55; adult students in, 49-62; attrition in, 56-57; participation in, 50-51; recruiting for, 51-53; responses of, 57-59, 95-97; summary on, 59-60. See also Continuing higher education
Hinings, C. R., 14, 22
Hirsh, J. B., 52, 61
Hodgkinson, H. L., 50, 51, 61
Hogan, T. P., 55, 61
Holt, M. E., 47, 48
Hong Kong, open university in, 91
Houle, C. O., 1, 2, 6, 10, 28, 32, 36, 48
Hu, M., 29-30, 32
Hull, W. L., 80, 81, 88
Human resources development (HRD): aspects of, 99-105; background on, 99; and needs assessment, 100-103; and recruitment, 103-104; summary on, 104

I

Illinois, marketing research in, 30
Illinois at Urbana-Champaign, University of, packaging at, 71
India, open university in, 91
Indonesia, open university in, 91
Information input, in organizations, 17-18
Instructional factors, and retention, 8-9
Integration, in organizations, 18
Intention, in participation model, 37-39, 41-42
Interpretive strategy: for recruitment, 69-70; and retention, 73-74
Involvement. See Participation
Iowa, University of, and distance education, 90
Israel, open university in, 91, 92
Italy, open university in, 91

J

Jaccard, J., 37, 48
Jackson, J. H., 17, 18, 22

James, B. J., 90, 98
Japan, open university in, 91
Jensen, D., 96, 98
Jensen, G., 8, 10
Johns Hopkins University, downtown center of, 58
Johnstone, J. W., 36, 48

K

Kahn, R. L., 14, 16, 22
Kast, F. E., 13-14, 19-20, 22
Katz, D., 14, 16, 22
Kentucky, University of, and distance education, 90
Kim, H. Y., 90, 97
Klus, J. P., 5, 7, 11
Knoll, J. H., 6, 10
Knowles, M. S., 5, 10, 20, 22
Knox, A. B., 68, 77
Kotler, P., 24-25, 27-28, 32, 83, 88

L

Lamoureux, M. E., 30, 32
Learning group. *See* Group experience
Lerche, R. S., 83, 85, 86, 87, 88
Life-style factors: and marketing, 29-30; typology of, and literacy programs, 81-82
Literacy and adult basic education: and age groups, 82; aspects of, 79-88; background on, 79-80; and lifestyles typology, 81-82; market research for, 83-84; need for, 80; promoting, 84-87; segmenting market for, 80-81; summary on, 87-88; targeting market for, 83
Locations, special, for adult students, 58
Long Island University C. W. Post Center, Women's Project at, 52
Loring, R. K., 64, 65, 71, 72, 75, 77
Ludlow, N., 91, 98
Lutz, R. J., 40, 48

M

McArdle, J. B., 40, 48
McDonald, J., 7, 10
Magarell, J., 50, 61

Malaney, G. D., 67, 68, 69, 77
Managerial subsystem, of organization, 20-21
Mark, M., 52, 59, 61
Marketing: applications of, 23-33; audits of, 25; background on, 23-24; concept of, 24; conclusions on, 31-32; and costs, 30; definition in, 26; and demand categories, 25-26; and design explanation, 29; and format description, 28; and leader selection, 28; and life-style factors, 29-30; and needs assessment, 27; orientations toward, 24-25; and participant roles and relationships, 29; and problem analysis, 27-28; and product, 27; and program planning, 24-28; and recruitment, 5-6, 28-31; research for, 83-84; research on, 30-31; and resource choice, 28; and retention, 31; and segmentation, 6, 26, 80-81; and social reinforcement, 28-29; and supportive publics, 30; targeting for, 83
Marsh-Williams, P., 54, 61
Martin, L. G., 2, 79-88
Maryland, University of, orientation by, 58
Mason, R. C., 28, 32
Meaning, managing, in continuing higher education, 73-74
Merriam, S. B., 70, 77
Metzner, B. S., 56, 57, 59, 60, 72, 74, 77
Mishler, C., 55, 61
Moore, M. G., 2, 65, 89-98
Moral involvement, 15-16, 21
Morgan, C. P., 17, 18, 22
Motivations: of adult students, 50-51, 64; and participation, 36; and recruitment, 6
Muhlenberg College, recruitment plan at, 52
Murgatroyd, S., 94, 98
Murphy, D. T., 52, 61

N

N. K. I. School (Norway), and retention, 93
National Home Study Council, 91

National Technological University, and distance education, 92
National University Continuing Education Association, 93
National University Teleconference Network, and distance education, 92
Needs assessment: for enhancing participation, 46; and human resources development, 100-103; and marketing, 27
Netherlands, open university in, 91
Networking, for literacy promotion, 86-87
Nevada, distance education in, 90
New Orleans, University of, downtown center of, 58
New York, distance education in, 90
Nicholson, E., 31, 32
Nicholson, N., 95, 98
Normative power, 14, 15-16, 21
Norms, subjective, 38-41, 44-46
North Island College (Canada), mobile study center of, 96
Norway, distance education in, 93
Nowlen, P. M., 65, 77

O

O'Connor, K., 51, 52, 61
Ohio University, Experiential Learning Program at, 52, 59
Olmsted, A. D., 90, 97
Open Learning Institute (Canada), and retention, 93
Open University (United Kingdom): correspondence education from, 90; history of, 91; open admission to, 92; recruitment and retention at, 93; student support services of, 95-96
Open-systems theory: and adaptive strategy, 67; concept of, 16; and organizational subsystems, 18-21; of organizations, 16-18
Organizational theory: applications of, 13-22; background on, 13-14; of compliance, 14-16; concept of, 13-14; of open systems, 16-18; on recruitment, 67-70; significance of, 21-22
Orientation program, for adult students, 58

Orientations, motivational, 6, 36
Otto, W., 31, 32
Outcomes, in participation model, 39-40, 42-44
Output, in organization, 17

P

Pakistan, open university in, 91
Paolillo, J.G.P., 17, 18, 22
Pappas, J. P., 64, 65, 71, 72, 75, 77
Parlett, M., 93, 94-95, 98
Participation: classes of, 14-16; in continuing higher education, 64, 65-67; and demand states, 83-84; enhancing, 46-47; in higher education, 50-51; increasing, 41-46; instrumental and expressive benefits of, 27; and marketing, 29; model for understanding, 37-41; motives for, 50-51, 64; program interface with, 65-67; rates of, 13; studies of, 35-37
Pennsylvania State University: and distance education, 90; orientation by, 58
Performance management system, in human resources development, 101-102
Perrino, D., 72, 77
Perry, R., 59, 61
Personal accommodation factors, and retention, 8
Personal contact, for literacy promotion, 86-87
Peters, T., 99, 105
Peterson, R., 13, 16, 22
Pfeiffer, J. W., 90, 98
Phillipp, J., 59, 61
Pitt Community College, and marketing, 5, 10, 52, 61
Planning: in human resources development, 100, 101, 103; program, 24-28, 70-71; strategic, 100; for succession, 101
Power, classes of, 14-16
Preadmission programs, for adult students, 58
Print media, for literacy promotion, 85
Professional education. See Continuing professional education

Program continuity: in continuing higher education, 66, 71; and retention, 9
Program planning: and marketing, 24-28; and recruitment, 70-71
Programs: participation interface with, 65-67; special, for adult students, 59
Promotion: function of, 24; of literacy programs, 84-87; and recruitment, 6-7
Pryor, B. W., 1, 35-48
Psychosocial subsystem, of organization, 20
Public Broadcasting Service, Adult Learning Service of, 92
Public relations, and recruitment, 5
Publicity, for literacy promotion, 87
Pugh, D. S., 14, 22

Q

Quigley, A., 83, 88

R

Ramsey, D., 5, 10
Ray, R. O., 40, 48
Recruitment: adaptive strategy for, 67-69; of adult students, 51-53; aspects of, 3-11; background on, 3-4; concept of, 3; in continuing higher education, 67-72; in continuing professional education, 35-48; in distance education, 89-98; guidelines for, 108; in higher education, 49-62; and human resources development, 103-104; interpretive strategy for, 67-70; in literacy and adult basic education, 79-88; and marketing, 5-6, 28-31; and organizational theory, 13-22, 67-70; packaging in, 71-72; practice of, 4-7; and program planning, 70-71; and promotion, 6-7; and public relations, 5; of right audience, 29; summary on, 9-10; and trajectory theory, 70-71
Regan, M. C., 58, 61
Remediation, for adult students, 59
Remunerative power, 14, 15
Resource-dependence theory, and adaptive strategy, 67

Retention: of adult students, 55-56, 57-59; aspects of, 3-11; background on, 3-4; and community of learners, 74-76; concept of, 3-4; in continuing higher education, 72-76; in continuing professional education, 35-48; in distance education, 89-98; guidelines for, 108-109; in higher education, 49-62; in literacy and adult basic education, 79-88; longitudinal and cross-sectional perspectives for, 73; and marketing, 31; and organizational theory, 13-22; practice of, 7-9; and reasons for attrition, 56-57, 94-95; summary on, 9-10
Rivera, R. J., 36, 48
Rodgers, M., 58, 61
Roelfs, P., 13, 16, 22
Rogers, E. M., 7, 10
Rosenzweig, J. E., 13-14, 19-20, 22
Ross, J. M., 2, 49-62
Rossi, K., 70, 71, 73, 77
Rubenson, K., 36, 48
Rumble, G., 91, 96, 98

S

Sabers, D., 90, 98
Sacramento City College, Continuing Education Program responsiveness in, 21-22
Saint Catherine College, preadmission predictors at, 54
Saint Peter's College, Public Policy program at, 59
Salter, D., 96, 98
Savarise, P., 91, 98
Scanlan, C. S., 36, 48, 68, 77
Scheduling, special, for adult students, 58
Schiamberg, L. B., 7, 11
Sechler, J. A., 80, 81, 88
Sections, special, for adult students, 58
Semlak, W. D., 55, 60
Sewall, T., 50-51, 61
Shipton, J., 58, 61
Sloan, D., 90, 98
Smith, A. D., 56, 61
Smith, F. B., 82, 88
Smith, J. W., 58, 61

Social composition, in continuing higher education, 66, 75
Social context, in continuing higher education, 65
Social contract: and recruitment, 69; and retention, 73-74
Social integration, in continuing higher education, 74
Social organization, in continuing higher education, 65-66, 75
Social reinforcement, and marketing, 28-29
Socially constructed reality, and recruitment, 69-70
South Carolina, University of, special sections at, 58
Spain, open university in, 91, 96
Spencer, O., 90, 98
Spiro, L. M., 53, 60, 70, 71, 73, 77
Sri Lanka, open university in, 91
State University of New York College at Brockport: recruitment survey at, 53; retention studies at, 73
Steady state, in organization, 18
Steltenpohl, E., 58, 61
Stern, M. R., 26-27, 32
Stock, W. P., 53, 60
Strategic planning, in human resources development, 100
Strother, G. B., 5, 7, 11
Structural subsystem, of organization, 19-20
Student support services: applications in distance education for, 90-98; function of, 92-93; history of, 90-92; as system response, 95-97
Students. *See* Adult students
Subjective norm: formation and change of, 44-46; in participation model, 38-41
Subsystems, organizational, 18-21
Succession planning, in human resources development, 101
Sugarman, M. N., 56, 61
Support groups, for adult students, 50
Suprasystem, concept of, 19
Surrey, D., 59, 61
Sy, M. J., 59, 61
System: concept of, 16; as cyclic, in organization, 17. *See also* Open-systems theory

T

Talbert, K., 63, 78
Task environment, and recruitment, 67-68
Technical subsystem, of organization, 19
Telemarketing, for literacy promotion, 87
Tennessee, University of, and distance education, 90
Test of Standard Written English, 54
Thailand, open university in, 91
Thieman, T., 54, 61
Thompson, C., 96, 98
Thompson, H. L., 52, 58, 61
Thompson, J. D., 67-69, 78
Throughput, in organization, 17
Trajectory theory, and recruiting, 70-71
Trist, E. L., 65, 77
Tyson, G. S., 59, 61

U

United Kingdom, Open University in, 90, 91, 92, 93, 95-96
United States Armed Forces Institute, dropouts from, 90

V

Valentine, T., 36, 48
Van Dyk, J., 51, 60
Venezuela, open university in, 91, 96

W

Washington, University of, and distance education, 90
Waterman, R., 99, 105
Wedemeyer, C., 90, 98
Weick, K. E., 66, 78
Weidman, J. C., 56, 61
Weinstein, L., 54-55, 62
Wheeler, S., 66, 78
White, C. J., 59, 62
Widener University, orientation by, 58
Wilcox, L., 55, 60
Willett, L. H., 70-71, 73, 78
Wisconsin, University of: admission

Wisconsin, University of *(continued)*
 Educational Counseling Service of, 96; correspondence courses from, 90
Wisconsin Assessment Center, 54, 62
Wisconsin-Milwaukee, University of, downtown center of, 58
Women, as adult students, 50, 52, 54–55

Woodley, A., 93, 94–95, 98
Woody, S., 55, 61
Wright State University, Family Life Education at, 59

Y

Yarosz, D. R., 2, 99–105